MznLnx

Missing Links Exam Preps

Exam Prep for

Environmental Geology

Montgomery, 6th Edition

The MznLnx Exam Prep is your link from the texbook and lecture to your exams.
The MznLnx Exam Preps are unauthorized and comprehensive reviews of your textbooks.

All material provided by MznLnx and Rico Publications (c) 2010
Textbook publishers and textbook authors do not particpate in or contribute to these reviews.

MznLnx

Rico Publications

Exam Prep for Environmental Geology
6th Edition
Montgomery

Publisher: Raymond Houge
Assistant Editor: Michael Rouger
Text and Cover Designer: Lisa Buckner
Marketing Manager: Sara Swagger
Project Manager, Editorial Production: Jerry Emerson
Art Director: Vernon Lowerui

Product Manager: Dave Mason
Editorial Assitant: Rachel Guzmanji
Pedagogy: Debra Long
Cover Image: Jim Reed/Getty Images
Text and Cover Printer: City Printing, Inc.
Compositor: Media Mix, Inc.

(c) 2010 Rico Publications
ALL RIGHTS RESERVED. No part of this work covered by the copyright may be reproduced or used in any form or by an means--graphic, electronic, or mechanical, including photocopying, recording, taping, Web distribution, information storage, and retrieval systems, or in any other manner--without the written permission of the publisher.

Printed in the United States
ISBN:

For more information about our products, contact us at:
Dave.Mason@RicoPublications.com

For permission to use material from this text or product, submit a request online to:
Dave.Mason@RicoPublications.com

Contents

CHAPTER 1
An Overview of Our Planetary Environment — 1

CHAPTER 2
Rocks and Minerals-A First Look — 7

CHAPTER 3
Plate Tectonics — 18

CHAPTER 4
Earthquakes — 27

CHAPTER 5
Volcanoes — 33

CHAPTER 6
Streams and Flooding — 42

CHAPTER 7
Coastal Zones and Processes — 47

CHAPTER 8
Mass Movements — 54

CHAPTER 9
Geology and Climate: Glaciers, Deserts, and Global Climate Trends — 60

CHAPTER 10
Water as a Resource — 69

CHAPTER 11
Soil as a Resource — 78

CHAPTER 12
Mineral and Rock Resources — 86

CHAPTER 13
Energy Resources-Fossil Fuels — 93

CHAPTER 14
Energy Resources-Alternative Sources — 101

CHAPTER 15
Waste Disposal — 107

CHAPTER 16
Water Pollution — 114

CHAPTER 17
Air Pollution — 121

CHAPTER 18
Environmental Law — 125

CHAPTER 19
Land-Use Planning and Engineering Geology — 131

ANSWER KEY — 137

TO THE STUDENT

COMPREHENSIVE

The *MznLnx* Exam Prep series is designed to help you pass your exams. Editors at MznLnx review your textbooks and then prepare these practice exams to help you master the textbook material. Unlike study guides, workbooks, and practice tests provided by the texbook publisher and textbook authors, *MznLnx* gives you **all** of the material in each chapter in exam form, not just samples, so you can be sure to nail your exam.

MECHANICAL

The MznLnx Exam Prep series creates exams that will help you learn the subject matter as well as test you on your understanding. Each question is designed to help you master the concept. Just working through the exams, you gain an understanding of the subject--its a simple mechanical process that produces success.

INTEGRATED STUDY GUIDE AND REVIEW

MznLnx is not just a set of exams designed to test you, its also a comprehensive review of the subject content. Each exam question is also a review of the concept, making sure that you will get the answer correct without having to go to other sources of material. You learn as you go! Its the easiest way to pass an exam.

HUMOR

Studying can be tedious and dry. MznLnx's instructional design includes moderate humor within the exam questions on occassion, to break the tedium and revitalize the brain

Chapter 1. An Overview of Our Planetary Environment   1

1. The _____ is a cosmological model of the initial conditions and subsequent development of the universe. It is supported by the most comprehensive and accurate explanations from current scientific evidence and observation. As used by cosmologists, the term _____ generally refers to the idea that the universe has expanded from a primordial hot and dense initial condition at some finite time in the past, and continues to expand to this day.

   a. 1700 Cascadia earthquake
   b. Big Bang
   c. 1509 Istanbul earthquake
   d. 1703 Genroku earthquake

2. The _____ or the Dirty Thirties was a period of severe dust storms causing major ecological and agricultural damage to American and Canadian prairie lands from 1930 to 1936 (in some areas until 1940.) The phenomenon was caused by severe drought coupled with decades of extensive farming without crop rotation or other techniques to prevent erosion. Deep plowing of the virgin topsoil of the Great Plains had killed the natural grasses that normally kept the soil in place and trapped moisture even during periods of drought and high winds.

   a. 1700 Cascadia earthquake
   b. 1509 Istanbul earthquake
   c. 1703 Genroku earthquake
   d. Dust Bowl

3. _____ is the geological process by which material is added to a landform or land mass. Fluids such as wind and water, as well as sediment gravity flows, transport previously eroded sediment, which, at the loss of enough kinetic energy in the fluid, is deposited, building up layers of sediment.

   _____ occurs when the forces responsible for sediment transportation are no longer sufficient to overcome the forces of particle weight and friction, which resist motion.

   a. Deposition
   b. Hydrothermal circulation
   c. Wave pounding
   d. Seafloor spreading

4. _____ is any particulate matter that can be transported by fluid flow, and which eventually is deposited.

   They are most often transported by water (fluvial processes) transported by wind (aeolian processes) and glaciers. Beach sands and river channel deposits are examples of fluvial transport and deposition, though _____ also often settles out of slow-moving or standing water in lakes and oceans.

   a. Fech fech
   b. Dry quicksand
   c. Sediment
   d. Brickearth

5. The _____ provides a uniform system of measuring pollution levels for the major air pollutants. It is based on a scale devised by the United States Environmental Protection Agency (USEPA) to provide a way for broadcasts and newspapers to report air quality on a daily basis.

   The _____ is reported as a number on a scale of 0 to 500 and is the air quality indicator.

   a. 1700 Cascadia earthquake
   b. 1509 Istanbul earthquake
   c. Pollutant Standards Index
   d. 1703 Genroku earthquake

6. _____ is the chemical element with the symbol Ca and atomic number 20. It has an atomic mass of 40.078 amu. _____ is a soft grey alkaline earth metal, and is the fifth most abundant element by mass in the Earth's crust.

Chapter 1. An Overview of Our Planetary Environment

    a. 1703 Genroku earthquake
    b. 1700 Cascadia earthquake
    c. 1509 Istanbul earthquake
    d. Calcium

7. _____ is a chemical element with the symbol Mg, atomic number 12, atomic weight 24.3050 and common oxidation number +2.

_____, an alkaline earth metal, is the ninth most abundant element in the universe by mass. The commonness of _____ is related to the fact that it is easily built up in supernova stars from a sequential addition of three helium nuclei to carbon .

    a. Magnesium
    b. 1509 Istanbul earthquake
    c. Pyrope
    d. Chromite

8. _____ is the part of Earth's lithosphere that surfaces in the ocean basins. _____ is primarily composed of mafic rocks, or sima. It is thinner than continental crust, or sial, generally less than 10 kilometers thick, however it is denser, having a mean density of about 3.3 grams per cubic centimeter.
    a. AL 129-1
    b. AASHTO Soil Classification System
    c. AL 333
    d. Oceanic crust

9. _____ is a chemical element. It has the symbol K , atomic number 19, and atomic mass 39.0983. _____ was first isolated from potash.
    a. 1509 Istanbul earthquake
    b. 1703 Genroku earthquake
    c. 1700 Cascadia earthquake
    d. Potassium

10. A _____ is a compound containing an anion in which one or more central silicon atoms are surrounded by electronegative ligands. This definition is broad enough to include species such as hexafluorosilicate ('fluorosilicate'), $[SiF_6]^{2-}$, but the _____ species that are encountered most often consist of silicon with oxygen as the ligand. _____ anions, with a negative net electrical charge, must have that charge balanced by other cations to make an electrically neutral compound.
    a. 1700 Cascadia earthquake
    b. 1509 Istanbul earthquake
    c. Silicate
    d. 1703 Genroku earthquake

11. A _____ is a mountain rising from the ocean seafloor that does not reach to the water's surface (sea level), and thus is not an island. These are typically formed from extinct volcanoes, that rise abruptly and are usually found rising from a seafloor of 1,000-4,000 meters depth. They are defined by oceanographers as independent features that rise to at least 1,000 meters above the seafloor.
    a. Seamount
    b. 1509 Istanbul earthquake
    c. 1703 Genroku earthquake
    d. 1700 Cascadia earthquake

12. _____, is a phylum of bacteria that obtain their energy through photosynthesis. The name '_____' comes from the color of the bacteria . They are a significant component of the marine nitrogen cycle and an important primary producer in many areas of the ocean, but are also found in habitats other than the marine environment; in particular _____ are known to occur in both freshwater, hypersaline inland lakes and in arid areas where they are a major component of biological soil crusts.

Chapter 1. An Overview of Our Planetary Environment 3

Stromatolites of fossilized oxygen-producing _____ have been found from 2.8 billion years ago. The ability of _____ to perform oxygenic photosynthesis is thought to have converted the early reducing atmosphere into an oxidizing one, which dramatically changed the composition of life forms on Earth by provoking an explosion of biodiversity and leading to the near-extinction of oxygen-intolerant organisms.

- a. 1509 Istanbul earthquake
- b. 1700 Cascadia earthquake
- c. Cyanobacteria
- d. 1703 Genroku earthquake

13. A _____, sometimes called a composite volcano, is a tall, conical volcano with many layers (strata) of hardened lava, tephra, and volcanic ash. They are characterized by a steep profile and periodic, explosive eruptions. The lava that flows from a _____ tends to be viscous; it cools and hardens before spreading far.
- a. Mount Overlord
- b. Stratovolcano
- c. Mount Baker
- d. Nevado Sajama

14. The _____ is a chronologic schema (or idealized model) relating stratigraphy to time that is used by geologists, paleontologists and other earth scientists to describe the timing and relationships between events that have occurred during the history of the Earth. The table of geologic time spans presented here agrees with the dates and nomenclature proposed by the International Commission on Stratigraphy, and uses the standard color codes of the United States Geological Survey.

Evidence from radiometric dating indicates that the Earth is about 4.570 billion years old.

- a. Geologic time scale
- b. 1700 Cascadia earthquake
- c. 1509 Istanbul earthquake
- d. 1703 Genroku earthquake

15. A _____ is an opening in a planet's surface or crust, which allows hot, molten rock, ash, and gases to escape from below the surface. Volcanic activity involving the extrusion of rock tends to form mountains or features like mountains over a period of time.
- a. Volcano
- b. 1509 Istanbul earthquake
- c. 1703 Genroku earthquake
- d. 1700 Cascadia earthquake

16. An _____ is the result of a sudden release of energy in the Earth's crust that creates seismic waves. They are recorded with a seismometer or the related and mostly obsolete Richter magnitude, with a magnitude 3 or lower _____ being mostly imperceptible and magnitude 7 causing serious damage over large areas.
- a. AL 333
- b. AL 129-1
- c. AASHTO Soil Classification System
- d. Earthquake

17. The _____ describes the continuous movement of water on, above, and below the surface of the Earth. Since the _____ is truly a 'cycle,' there is no beginning or end. Water can change states among liquid, vapor, and ice at various places in the _____.
- a. Specific storage
- b. Surface water
- c. Hydraulic conductivity
- d. Water cycle

18. _____, also known as open-cast mining, open-cut mining, and strip mining, refers to a method of extracting rock or minerals from the earth by their removal from an open pit or borrow.

The term is used to differentiate this form of mining from extractive methods that require tunneling into the earth. Open-pit mines are used when deposits of commercially useful minerals or rock are found near the surface; that is, where the overburden is relatively thin or the material of interest is structurally unsuitable for tunneling

   a. AL 129-1
   b. AASHTO Soil Classification System
   c. Open-pit mining
   d. AL 333

19. A _____ zone or _____ area is the interface between land and a stream. Plant communities along the river margins are called _____ vegetation, characterized by hydrophilic plants. _____ zones are significant in ecology, environmental management, and civil engineering because of their role in soil conservation, their biodiversity, and the influence they have on aquatic ecosystems.
   a. 1509 Istanbul earthquake
   b. 1703 Genroku earthquake
   c. 1700 Cascadia earthquake
   d. Riparian

20. The _____ is a fundamental concept in geology that describes the dynamic transitions through geologic time among the three main rock types: sedimentary, metamorphic, and igneous. Each type of rock is altered or destroyed when it is forced out of its equilibrium conditions. An igneous rock such as basalt may break down and dissolve when exposed to the atmosphere, or melt as it is subducted under a continent.
   a. Serpentinite
   b. Metamorphic rock
   c. Metavolcanic rock
   d. Rock cycle

21. _____ is a sedimentary rock composed mainly of sand-size mineral or rock grains. Most _____ is composed of quartz and/or feldspar because these are the most common minerals in the Earth's crust. Like sand, _____ may be any color, but the most common colors are tan, brown, yellow, red, gray and white.
   a. Keystone
   b. Porcellanite
   c. Lithification
   d. Sandstone

22. _____ is the movement of the Earth's continents relative to each other. The hypothesis that continents 'drift' was first put forward by Abraham Ortelius in 1596 and was fully developed by Alfred Wegener in 1912. However, it was not until the development of the theory of plate tectonics in the 1960s, that a sufficient geological explanation of that movement was found.
   a. Continental drift
   b. Subduction
   c. Thrust fault
   d. Plate tectonics

23. In geology, _____ is transported rock debris overlying the solid bedrock. The term is also sometimes refers to organic debris so-transported. In the largest sense, it refers to the material left behind by retreating continental glaciers.
   a. Duricrust
   b. Gibraltar Arc
   c. Fulgurites
   d. Drift

24. _____ circulation in its most general sense is the circulation of hot water; 'hydros' in the Greek meaning water and 'thermos' meaning heat. _____ circulation occurs most often in the vicinity of sources of heat within the Earth's crust. This generally occurs near volcanic activity, but can occur in the deep crust related to the intrusion of granite, or as the result of orogeny or metamorphism.
   a. Seafloor spreading
   b. Stoping
   c. Permineralization
   d. Hydrothermal

Chapter 1. An Overview of Our Planetary Environment 5

25. A _____ or sandbar is a somewhat linear landform within or extending into a body of water, typically composed of sand, silt or small pebbles. A bar is characteristically long and narrow and develops where a stream or ocean current promotes deposition of granular material, resulting in localized shallowing of the water. Bars can appear in the sea, in a lake, or in a river.

The term _____ can be applied to larger geological units that form off a coastline as part of the process of coastal erosion. These include spits and baymouth bars that form across the front of embayments and rias. A tombolo is a bar that forms an isthmus between an island or offshore rock and a mainland shore.

  a. 1703 Genroku earthquake   b. 1700 Cascadia earthquake
  c. 1509 Istanbul earthquake   d. Shoal

26. _____ is a process that converts carbonaceous materials, such as coal, petroleum, biofuel into carbon monoxide and hydrogen by reacting the raw material at high temperatures with a controlled amount of oxygen and/or steam. The resulting gas mixture is called synthesis gas or syngas and is itself a fuel. _____ is a method for extracting energy from many different types of organic materials.

  a. 1509 Istanbul earthquake   b. 1700 Cascadia earthquake
  c. 1703 Genroku earthquake   d. Gasification

27. The _____ of a biological species in an environment is the population size of the species that the environment can sustain in the long term, given the food, habitat, water and other necessities available in the environment. For the human population, more complex variables such as sanitation and medical care are sometimes considered as part of the necessary infrastructure.

As population density increases, birth rate often increases and death rate typically decreases.

  a. 1703 Genroku earthquake   b. 1509 Istanbul earthquake
  c. 1700 Cascadia earthquake   d. Carrying capacity

28. _____ is the removal of solids (sediment, soil, rock and other particles) in the natural environment. It usually occurs due to transport by wind, water, or ice; by down-slope creep of soil and other material under the force of gravity; or by living organisms, such as burrowing animals, in the case of bioerosion.

_____ is distinguished from weathering, which is the process of chemical or physical breakdown of the minerals in the rocks, although the two processes may occur concurrently.

  a. Erosion   b. AASHTO Soil Classification System
  c. AL 129-1   d. AL 333

29. In geology, a _____ or _____ line is a planar fracture in rock in which the rock on one side of the fracture has moved with respect to the rock on the other side. Large _____s within the Earth's crust are the result of differential or shear motion and active _____ zones are the causal locations of most earthquakes. Earthquakes are caused by energy release during rapid slippage along a _____.

  a. Stack   b. Streak
  c. Tarn   d. Fault

30. A _____ is a geological phenomenon which includes a wide range of ground movement, such as rock falls, deep failure of slopes and shallow debris flows, which can occur in offshore, coastal and onshore environments. Although the action of gravity is the primary driving force for a _____ to occur, there are other contributing factors affecting the original slope stability. Typically, pre-conditional factors build up specific sub-surface conditions that make the area/slope prone to failure, whereas the actual _____ often requires a trigger before being released.
   a. 1509 Istanbul earthquake
   b. Mass wasting
   c. 1700 Cascadia earthquake
   d. Landslide

Chapter 2. Rocks and Minerals-A First Look

1. _____ are type of elastic wave, also called seismic waves, that can travel through gases, elastic solids and liquids, including the Earth. _____ can be produced by earthquakes and recorded by seismometers.

   a. P-waves
   b. 1509 Istanbul earthquake
   c. 1703 Genroku earthquake
   d. 1700 Cascadia earthquake

2. _____ is the second most abundant mineral in the Earth's continental crust. It is made up of a framework of silicon-oxygen tetrahedra SiO_4, with each silicon shared between two oxygens to give the overall formula SiO_2. _____ has a hardness of 7 on the Mohs scale and a density of 2.65 g/cmÂ³.

   a. 1703 Genroku earthquake
   b. Quartz
   c. 1509 Istanbul earthquake
   d. 1700 Cascadia earthquake

3. The _____ is a key axiom based on observations of natural history that is a foundational principle of sedimentary stratigraphy and so of other geology dependent natural sciences: 'Sedimentary layers are deposited in a time sequence, with the oldest on the bottom and the youngest on the top.'

   The principle was first proposed in the 11th century by the Persian geologist, Avicenna, and the law was later formulated more clearly in the 17th century by the Danish scientist Nicolas Steno.

   While discussing the origins of mountains in The Book of Healing in 1027, Avicenna first outlined the principle of the superposition of strata.

   a. Law of superposition
   b. Stage
   c. Chronostratigraphy
   d. Lichenometry

4. A _____ is a free neutron that is Boltzmann distributed with kT = 0.024 eV (4.0×10^{-21} J) at room temperature. This gives characteristic (not average, or median) speed of 2.2 km/s. The name 'thermal' comes from their energy being that of the room temperature gas or material they are permeating.

   a. 1703 Genroku earthquake
   b. 1700 Cascadia earthquake
   c. 1509 Istanbul earthquake
   d. Thermal neutron

5. A covalent bond is a form of chemical bonding that is characterized by the sharing of pairs of electrons between atoms, or between atoms and other covalent bonds. In short, attraction-to-repulsion stability that forms between atoms when they share electrons is known as _____.

   _____ includes many kinds of interaction, including >σ-bonding, >π-bonding, metal to non-metal bonding, agostic interactions, and three-center two-electron bonds.

   a. 1509 Istanbul earthquake
   b. 1700 Cascadia earthquake
   c. 1703 Genroku earthquake
   d. Covalent bonding

6. In geology, _____ refers to heat sources within the planet. _____ is technically an adjective (e.g., _____ energy) but in U.S. English the word has attained frequent use as a noun.

   The planet's internal heat was originally generated during its accretion, due to gravitational binding energy, and since then additional heat has continued to be generated by decay heat from the radioactive decay of elements.

Chapter 2. Rocks and Minerals-A First Look

    a. Diamond Head   b. Fault
    c. Platform   d. Geothermal

7. An _____ is a type of chemical bond that involves a metal and a non-metal ion (or polyatomic ions such as ammonium) through electrostatic attraction. In short, it is a bond formed by the attraction between two oppositely charged ions. The metal donates one or more electrons, forming a positively charged ion or cation with a stable electron configuration.
    a. AASHTO Soil Classification System   b. Ionic bond
    c. AL 129-1   d. AL 333

8. In mineralogy and crystallography, a _____ is a unique arrangement of atoms in a crystal. A _____ is composed of a motif, a set of atoms arranged in a particular way, and a lattice. Motifs are located upon the points of a lattice, which is an array of points repeating periodically in three dimensions.
    a. Crystal structure   b. 1509 Istanbul earthquake
    c. 1703 Genroku earthquake   d. 1700 Cascadia earthquake

9. A _____ or sandbar is a somewhat linear landform within or extending into a body of water, typically composed of sand, silt or small pebbles. A bar is characteristically long and narrow and develops where a stream or ocean current promotes deposition of granular material, resulting in localized shallowing of the water. Bars can appear in the sea, in a lake, or in a river.

The term _____ can be applied to larger geological units that form off a coastline as part of the process of coastal erosion. These include spits and baymouth bars that form across the front of embayments and rias. A tombolo is a bar that forms an isthmus between an island or offshore rock and a mainland shore.

    a. 1703 Genroku earthquake   b. Shoal
    c. 1700 Cascadia earthquake   d. 1509 Istanbul earthquake

10. _____ is a crystalline form of aluminium oxide (>α-Al_2O_3) and is one of the rock-forming minerals. It is naturally clear, but can have different colors when impurities are present. Transparent specimens are used as gems, called ruby if red, while all other colors are called sapphire.
    a. Corundum   b. 1700 Cascadia earthquake
    c. 1509 Istanbul earthquake   d. 1703 Genroku earthquake

11. _____ is a mineral composed of calcium fluoride, CaF_2. It is an isometric mineral with a cubic habit, though octahedral and more complex isometric forms are not uncommon. Cubic crystals up to 20 cm across have been found at Dalnegorsk, Russia.

_____ may occur as a vein deposit, especially with metallic minerals, where it often forms a part of the gangue (the worthless 'host-rock' in which valuable minerals occur) and may be associated with galena, sphalerite, barite, quartz, and calcite. It is a common mineral in deposits of hydrothermal origin and has been noted as a primary mineral in granites and other igneous rocks and as a common minor constituent of dolostone and limestone.

Chapter 2. Rocks and Minerals-A First Look

a. 1700 Cascadia earthquake
b. 1509 Istanbul earthquake
c. 1703 Genroku earthquake
d. Fluorite

12. A _____ is a mountain rising from the ocean seafloor that does not reach to the water's surface (sea level), and thus is not an island. These are typically formed from extinct volcanoes, that rise abruptly and are usually found rising from a seafloor of 1,000-4,000 meters depth. They are defined by oceanographers as independent features that rise to at least 1,000 meters above the seafloor.

a. 1703 Genroku earthquake
b. Seamount
c. 1509 Istanbul earthquake
d. 1700 Cascadia earthquake

13. A _____ is a pink to blood-red gemstone, a variety of the mineral corundum (aluminium oxide.) The red color is caused mainly by the presence of the element chromium. Its name comes from ruber, Latin for red.

a. 1703 Genroku earthquake
b. 1509 Istanbul earthquake
c. 1700 Cascadia earthquake
d. Ruby

14. The _____ characterizes the scratch resistance of various minerals through the ability of a harder material to scratch a softer material. It was created in 1812 by the German mineralogist Friedrich Mohs and is one of several definitions of hardness in materials science. The method, however, is of great antiquity, having first been mentioned by Theophrastus in his treatise On Stones in ca 300 BC, followed by Pliny the Elder in his Naturalis Historia circa A.D.

a. 1703 Genroku earthquake
b. 1700 Cascadia earthquake
c. 1509 Istanbul earthquake
d. Mohs scale of mineral hardness

15. _____ is a group of phosphate minerals, usually referring to hydroxylapatite, fluorapatite, and chlorapatite $F^{>-}$, or $Cl^{>-}$ ions, respectively, in the crystal. The formula of the admixture of the three most common endmembers is written as $Ca_5(PO_4)_3(OH, F, Cl)$, and the formulae of the individual minerals are written as $Ca_5(PO_4)_3(OH)$, $Ca_5(PO_4)_3F$ and $Ca_5(PO_4)_3Cl$, respectively.

_____ is one of few minerals that are produced and used by biological micro-environmental systems.

a. Apatite
b. AASHTO Soil Classification System
c. AL 129-1
d. AL 333

16. _____, in structural geology and related disciplines, describes the tendency of a rock to break along preferred planes of weakness.

Rocks deformed under very low to low metamorphic grade often develop planes along which the rock can easily be split. Slates are an example of a rock with a penetrative _____ caused partly by the realignment of phyllosilicate minerals with increasing flattening strain.

a. Platform
b. Stratification
c. Drainage system
d. Cleavage

17. _____ is an important tectosilicate mineral which forms igneous rock. The name is from the Greek for 'straight fracture,' because its two cleavage planes are at right angles to each other. An alternate name is alkali feldspar.

_____ is a common constituent of most granites and other felsic igneous rocks and often forms huge crystals and masses in pegmatite.

a. AL 129-1
b. AASHTO Soil Classification System
c. Orthoclase
d. AL 333

18. _____ is a mineral composed of hydrated magnesium silicate with the chemical formula H_2Mg_{34} or $Mg_3Si_4O_{10}(OH)_2$. In loose form, it is the widely used substance known as talcum powder. It occurs as foliated to fibrous masses, its monoclinic crystals being so rare as to be almost unknown.

_____ is a metamorphic mineral resulting from the metamorphism of magnesian minerals such as pyroxene, amphibole, olivine and other similar minerals in the presence of carbon dioxide and water. This is known as _____ carbonation or steatization and produces a suite of rocks known as _____ carbonates.

a. 1703 Genroku earthquake
b. 1700 Cascadia earthquake
c. 1509 Istanbul earthquake
d. Talc

19. A _____ is an opening in a planet's surface or crust, which allows hot, molten rock, ash, and gases to escape from below the surface. Volcanic activity involving the extrusion of rock tends to form mountains or features like mountains over a period of time.

a. 1700 Cascadia earthquake
b. Volcano
c. 1703 Genroku earthquake
d. 1509 Istanbul earthquake

20. _____ is a naturally occurring material composed primarily of fine-grained minerals, which show plasticity through a variable range of water content, and which can be hardened when dried and/or fired. _____ deposits are mostly composed of _____ minerals (phyllosilicate minerals), minerals which impart plasticity and harden when fired and/or dried, and variable amounts of water trapped in the mineral structure by polar attraction. Organic materials which do not impart plasticity may also be a part of _____ deposits.

a. 1700 Cascadia earthquake
b. 1509 Istanbul earthquake
c. 1703 Genroku earthquake
d. Clay

21. _____ are a group of rock-forming tectosilicate minerals which make up as much as 60% of the Earth's crust.

_____ crystallize from magma in both intrusive and extrusive igneous rocks, as veins, and are also present in many types of metamorphic rock. Rock formed entirely of plagioclase feldspar is known as anorthosite.

a. Feldspars
b. 1703 Genroku earthquake
c. 1700 Cascadia earthquake
d. 1509 Istanbul earthquake

22. The mineral _____ is a magnesium iron silicate with the formula $(Mg,Fe)_2SiO_4$. It is one of the most common minerals on Earth, and has also been identified in meteorites and on the Moon, Mars, and comet Wild 2.

The ratio of magnesium and iron varies between the two endmembers of the solid solution series: forsterite (Mg-endmember) and fayalite (Fe-endmember.)

a. AL 129-1 b. AL 333
c. AASHTO Soil Classification System d. Olivine

23. A _____ is a compound containing an anion in which one or more central silicon atoms are surrounded by electronegative ligands. This definition is broad enough to include species such as hexafluorosilicate ('fluorosilicate'), $[SiF_6]^{2-}$, but the _____ species that are encountered most often consist of silicon with oxygen as the ligand. _____ anions, with a negative net electrical charge, must have that charge balanced by other cations to make an electrically neutral compound.
   a. 1700 Cascadia earthquake b. 1509 Istanbul earthquake
   c. Silicate d. 1703 Genroku earthquake

24. In chemistry, a _____ is a salt or ester of carbonic acid.

To test for the presence of the _____ anion in a salt, the addition of dilute mineral acid (e.g. hydrochloric acid) will yield carbon dioxide gas.

_____-containing salts are industrially and mineralogically ubiquitous.

   a. 1703 Genroku earthquake b. 1700 Cascadia earthquake
   c. Carbonate d. 1509 Istanbul earthquake

25. A _____ is a binary compound, of which one part is a halogen atom and the other part is an element or radical that is less electronegative than the halogen, to make a fluoride, chloride, bromide, iodide, or astatide compound. Many salts are _____s. All Group 1 metals form _____s with the halogens and they are white solids.
   a. 1700 Cascadia earthquake b. 1703 Genroku earthquake
   c. Halide d. 1509 Istanbul earthquake

26. In inorganic chemistry, a _____ is a salt of sulfuric acid.

The _____ ion is a polyatomic anion with the empirical formula SO_4^{2-} and a molecular mass of 96.06 daltons; it consists of a central sulfur atom surrounded by four equivalent oxygen atoms in a tetrahedral arrangement. The sulfur atom is in the +6 oxidation state while the four oxygen atoms are each in the -2 state.

   a. 1703 Genroku earthquake b. Sulfate
   c. 1700 Cascadia earthquake d. 1509 Istanbul earthquake

27. A _____ zone or _____ area is the interface between land and a stream. Plant communities along the river margins are called _____ vegetation, characterized by hydrophilic plants. _____ zones are significant in ecology, environmental management, and civil engineering because of their role in soil conservation, their biodiversity, and the influence they have on aquatic ecosystems.
   a. Riparian b. 1509 Istanbul earthquake
   c. 1703 Genroku earthquake d. 1700 Cascadia earthquake

28. _____ is the name of a sedimentary carbonate rock and a mineral, both composed of calcium magnesium carbonate $CaMg_2$ found in crystals.

_____ rock (also dolostone) is composed predominantly of the mineral _____. Limestone that is partially replaced by _____ is referred to as dolomitic limestone, or in old U.S. geologic literature as magnesian limestone.

a. Dolomite
b. Metasediment
c. Jasperoid
d. Sedimentary deposits

29. _____ or loadstone refers to naturally occurring pieces of intensely magnetic magnetite that were used for magnetizing compasses.

Iron, steel and ordinary magnetite are attracted to a magnetic field, including the Earth's magnetic field. Only magnetite with a particular crystalline structure, _____, has the coercivity to act as a permanent magnet and attract and magnetize iron. The naturally occurring specimens are magnetized by the strong fields surrounding lightning bolts.

a. 1700 Cascadia earthquake
b. 1509 Istanbul earthquake
c. 1703 Genroku earthquake
d. Lodestone

30. _____ or white asbestos is the most commonly encountered form of asbestos, accounting for approximately 95% of the asbestos in place in the United States and a similar proportion in other countries. It is a soft, fibrous silicate mineral in the serpentine group of phyllosilicates: as such, it is distinct from other asbestiform minerals in the amphibole group. Its idealized chemical formula is $Mg_3(Si_2O_5)(OH)_4$, in which some of the magnesium ions may be substituted by iron or other cations.

a. Kaolinite
b. 1509 Istanbul earthquake
c. 1700 Cascadia earthquake
d. Chrysotile

31. _____ was a supercontinent that most recently existed as a part of the split of the Pangaean supercontinent in the late Mesozoic era. It included most of the landmasses which make up today's continents of the northern hemisphere, chiefly Laurentia (the name given to the North American craton), Baltica, Siberia, Kazakhstania, and the North China and East China cratons.

a. 1700 Cascadia earthquake
b. Rodinia
c. 1509 Istanbul earthquake
d. Laurasia

32. The _____ Era is one of three geologic eras of the Phanerozoic eon. The division of time into eras dates back to Giovanni Arduino, in the 18th century, although his original name for the era now called the '_____' was 'Secondary' (making the modern era the 'Tertiary'.)

The _____ was a time of tectonic, climatic and evolutionary activity. The continents gradually shifted from a state of connectedness into their present configuration; the drifting provided for speciation and other important evolutionary developments.

a. 1703 Genroku earthquake
b. 1700 Cascadia earthquake
c. 1509 Istanbul earthquake
d. Mesozoic

Chapter 2. Rocks and Minerals-A First Look

33. The _____ is the epoch from 1.8 million to 11550 years BP covering the world's recent period of repeated glaciations. The _____ epoch follows the Pliocene epoch and is followed by the Holocene epoch. The _____ is the third epoch of the Neogene period or 6th epoch of the Cenozoic Era. The end of the _____ corresponds with the retreat of the last continental glacier. It also corresponds with the end of the Paleolithic age used in archaeology.
    a. Tyrrhenian
    b. Sicilian Stage
    c. Pleistocene
    d. Late Pleistocene

34. _____, also known as the Pleistocene glaciation, the current ice age or simply the ice age, refers to the period of the last few million years in which permanent ice sheets were established in Antarctica and perhaps Greenland, and fluctuating ice sheets have occurred elsewhere The major effects of the ice age were erosion and deposition of material over large parts of the continents, modification of river systems, creation of millions of lakes, changes in sea level, development of pluvial lakes far from the ice margins, isostatic adjustment of the crust, and abnormal winds. It affected oceans, flooding, and biological communities.
    a. Glacial period
    b. Wolstonian Stage
    c. Quaternary glaciation
    d. Bergschrund

35. The _____ was proposed by the Danish geological pioneer Nicholas Steno (1638-1686.) This principle states that layers of sediment are originally deposited horizontally. The principle is important to the analysis of folded and tilted strata.
    a. Cyclostratigraphy
    b. Principle of Original Horizontality
    c. Bedrock
    d. Key bed

36. Volatile organic compounds (_____) are gases or vapours emitted by various solids or liquids, many of which have short- and long-term adverse health effects. Household products that emit _____ include paint, paint strippers, cleaning supplies, pesticides, glues and adhesives, building materials and furnishings. Consequently, concentrations of many _____ are higher indoors (up to ten times higher) than outdoors.
    a. 1700 Cascadia earthquake
    b. 1509 Istanbul earthquake
    c. 1703 Genroku earthquake
    d. VOCs

37. _____ is one of the three main rock types (the others being sedimentary and metamorphic rock.) _____ is formed by magma (molten rock) being cooled and becoming solid . They may form with or without crystallization, either below the surface as intrusive (plutonic) rocks or on the surface as extrusive (volcanic) rocks. They make up approximately 95% of the upper part of the Earth's crust, but their great abundance is hidden on the Earth's surface by a relatively thin but widespread layer of sedimentary and metamorphic rocks.
    a. AASHTO Soil Classification System
    b. AL 129-1
    c. AL 333
    d. Igneous rock

38. _____ is molten rock that is found beneath the surface of the Earth, and may also exist on other terrestrial planets. Besides molten rock, _____ may also contain suspended crystals and gas bubbles. _____ often collects in a _____ chamber inside a volcano. _____ is capable of intrusion into adjacent rocks, extrusion onto the surface as lava, and explosive ejection as tephra to form pyroclastic rock.
    a. Pluton
    b. Laccolith
    c. Volcanic rock
    d. Magma

39. A _____ is a large emplacement of igneous intrusive rock that forms from cooled magma deep in the Earth's crust. they are almost always made mostly of felsic or intermediate rock-types, such as granite, quartz monzonite, or diorite

Although they may appear uniform, _____s are in fact structures with complex histories and compositions.

a. Flood basalt
b. Coldwell Complex
c. Pyroclastic rocks
d. Batholith

40. The _____ is a fundamental concept in geology that describes the dynamic transitions through geologic time among the three main rock types: sedimentary, metamorphic, and igneous. Each type of rock is altered or destroyed when it is forced out of its equilibrium conditions. An igneous rock such as basalt may break down and dissolve when exposed to the atmosphere, or melt as it is subducted under a continent.

a. Metamorphic rock
b. Serpentinite
c. Rock cycle
d. Metavolcanic rock

41. _____ is an igneous rock of volcanic origin.

They are usually fine-grained or aphanitic to glassy in texture. They often contain clasts of other rocks and phenocrysts.

a. Metavolcanic rock
b. Magma
c. Pluton
d. Volcanic rock

42. The _____ provides a uniform system of measuring pollution levels for the major air pollutants. It is based on a scale devised by the United States Environmental Protection Agency (USEPA) to provide a way for broadcasts and newspapers to report air quality on a daily basis.

The _____ is reported as a number on a scale of 0 to 500 and is the air quality indicator.

a. 1509 Istanbul earthquake
b. 1700 Cascadia earthquake
c. 1703 Genroku earthquake
d. Pollutant Standards Index

43. _____ is a common extrusive volcanic rock. It is usually grey to black and fine-grained due to rapid cooling of lava at the surface of a planet. It may be porphyritic containing larger crystals in a fine matrix, or vesicular, or frothy scoria.

a. 1703 Genroku earthquake
b. 1700 Cascadia earthquake
c. 1509 Istanbul earthquake
d. Basalt

44. _____ is a naturally occurring glass formed as an extrusive igneous rock. It is produced when felsic lava extruded from a volcano cools without crystal growth. _____ is commonly found within the margins of rhyolitic lava flows known as _____ flows, where the chemical composition (high silica content) induces a high viscosity and polymerization degree of the lava.

a. AL 333
b. AL 129-1
c. AASHTO Soil Classification System
d. Obsidian

45. _____ rocks are composed of fragments of pre-existing rock. The term is most commonly, but not uniquely, applied to sedimentary rocks.

_____ metamorphic rocks include breccias formed in faults, as well as some protomylonite and pseudotachylite.

   a. 1703 Genroku earthquake
   b. 1700 Cascadia earthquake
   c. Clastic
   d. 1509 Istanbul earthquake

46. A _____ is a rock consisting of individual stones that have become cemented together. They are sedimentary rocks consisting of rounded fragments and are thus differentiated from breccias, which consist of angular clasts. Both _____s and breccias are characterized by clasts larger than sand (>2 mm).
   a. Dolostone
   b. Conglomerate
   c. Superficial deposits
   d. Porcellanite

47. An _____ is the result of a sudden release of energy in the Earth's crust that creates seismic waves. They are recorded with a seismometer or the related and mostly obsolete Richter magnitude, with a magnitude 3 or lower _____ being mostly imperceptible and magnitude 7 causing serious damage over large areas.
   a. AASHTO Soil Classification System
   b. AL 129-1
   c. AL 333
   d. Earthquake

48. _____ is the process in which sediments compact under pressure, expel connate fluids, and gradually become solid rock. Essentially, _____ is a process of porosity destruction through compaction and cementation. _____ includes all the processes which convert unconsolidated sediments into sedimentary rocks.
   a. Metasediment
   b. Pelagic sediments
   c. Porcellanite
   d. Lithification

49. _____ is a sedimentary rock composed mainly of sand-size mineral or rock grains. Most _____ is composed of quartz and/or feldspar because these are the most common minerals in the Earth's crust. Like sand, _____ may be any color, but the most common colors are tan, brown, yellow, red, gray and white.
   a. Lithification
   b. Keystone
   c. Porcellanite
   d. Sandstone

50. _____ is one of the three main rock types (the others being igneous and metamorphic rock.) _____ is formed by deposition and consolidation of mineral and organic material and from precipitation of minerals from solution. The processes that form _____ occur at the surface of the Earth and within bodies of water.
   a. Vesicular texture
   b. Sedimentary rock
   c. Pluton
   d. Laccolith

51. _____ is a fine-grained sedimentary rock whose original constituents were clay minerals or muds. It is characterized by thin laminae breaking with an irregular curving fracture, often splintery and usually parallel to the often-indistinguishable bedding plane. This property is called fissility.
   a. Dolomite
   b. Mudstone
   c. Shale
   d. Porcellanite

Chapter 2. Rocks and Minerals-A First Look

52. _____ is the naturally occurring, unconsolidated or loose covering on the Earth's surface. _____ is composed of particles of broken rock that have been altered by chemical, biological and environmental processes including weathering and erosion. _____ is different from its parent rock(s) source(s), altered by interactions between the lithosphere, hydrosphere, atmosphere, and the biosphere.
   a. Slump
   c. 1509 Istanbul earthquake
   b. Topsoil
   d. Soil

53. _____ is a sedimentary rock composed largely of the mineral calcite (calcium carbonate: $CaCO_3$.) The deposition of _____ strata is often a by-product and indicator of biological activity in the geologic record. Calcium (along with nitrogen, phosphorus, and potassium) is a key mineral to plant nutrition: soils overlying _____ bedrock tend to be pre-fertilized with calcium.
   a. 1703 Genroku earthquake
   c. 1509 Istanbul earthquake
   b. Limestone
   d. 1700 Cascadia earthquake

54. _____ is the largest and best-known genus of the extinct order of seed ferns known as Glossopteridales (or in some cases as Arberiales or Dictyopteridiales.)

The Glossopteridales arose around the beginning of the Permian on the great southern continent of Gondwana. These plants went on to become the dominant elements of the southern flora through the rest of the Permian but disappeared in almost all places at the end of the Permian.

   a. Glossopteris
   c. 1509 Istanbul earthquake
   b. Pteridospermatophyta
   d. Petrified wood

55. _____ is a common and widely distributed type of rock formed by high-grade regional metamorphic processes from pre-existing formations that were originally either igneous or sedimentary rocks. Gneissic rocks are usually medium to coarse foliated and largely recrystallized but do not carry large quantities of micas, chlorite or other platy minerals. _____ es that are metamorphosed igneous rocks or their equivalent are termed granite _____ es, diorite _____ es, etc.
   a. 1703 Genroku earthquake
   c. 1700 Cascadia earthquake
   b. Gneiss
   d. 1509 Istanbul earthquake

56. _____ is the result of the transformation of an existing rock type, the protolith, in a process called metamorphism, which means 'change in form'. The protolith is subjected to heat and pressure (temperatures greater than 150 to 200 >°C and pressures of 1500 bars) causing profound physical and/or chemical change. The protolith may be sedimentary rock, igneous rock or another older _____.
   a. Serpentinite
   c. Metamorphic rock
   b. Rock cycle
   d. Metavolcanic rock

57. _____ is a hard metamorphic rock which was originally sandstone. Sandstone is converted into _____ through heating and pressure usually related to tectonic compression within orogenic belts. Pure _____ is usually white to grey, though _____ s often occur in various shades of pink and red due to varying amounts of iron oxide .
   a. Quartzite
   c. Facies
   b. Cataclasite
   d. Mylonite

58. _____ forms a group of medium-grade metamorphic rocks, chiefly notable for the preponderance of lamellar minerals such as micas, chlorite, talc, hornblende, graphite, and others. Quartz often occurs in drawn-out grains to such an extent that a particular form called quartz _____ is produced. By definition, _____ contains more than 50% platy and elongated minerals, often finely interleaved with quartz and feldspar.
   a. Metaconglomerate
   b. Schist
   c. Jadeitite
   d. Greenschist

59. _____ is any penetrative planar fabric present in rocks. _____ is common to rocks affected by regional metamorphic compression typical of orogenic belts. Rocks exhibiting _____ include the typical metamorphic rock sequence of slate, phyllite, schist and gneiss.
   a. Hornfels
   b. Foliation
   c. Greenschist
   d. Quartzite

60. _____ is the solid-state recrystallization of pre-existing rocks due to changes in physical and chemical conditions, primarily heat, pressure, and the introduction of chemically active fluids. Both mineralogical, chemical and crystallographic changes can occur during this process.

Three types of _____ exist: dynamic, contact and regional.

   a. Gibraltar Arc
   b. Pumice raft
   c. Lake capture
   d. Metamorphism

61. _____ is soil or rock derived granular material of a grain size between sand and clay. _____ may occur as a soil or as suspended sediment in a surface water body. It may also exist as soil deposited at the bottom of a water body.
   a. 1509 Istanbul earthquake
   b. Silt
   c. 1703 Genroku earthquake
   d. 1700 Cascadia earthquake

62. _____ is a fine-grained, foliated, homogeneous metamorphic rock derived from an original shale-type sedimentary rock composed of clay or volcanic ash through low grade regional metamorphism. The result is a foliated rock in which the foliation may not correspond to the original sedimentary layering. _____ is frequently grey in colour especially when seen en masse covering roofs.
   a. Shock metamorphism
   b. Mylonite
   c. Metaconglomerate
   d. Slate

Chapter 3. Plate Tectonics

1. The _____, also known as the local magnitude (M_L) scale, assigns a single number to quantify the amount of seismic energy released by an earthquake. It is a base-10 logarithmic scale obtained by calculating the logarithm of the combined horizontal amplitude of the largest displacement from zero on a Wood-Anderson torsion seismometer output. So, for example, an earthquake that measures 5.0 on the Richter scale has a shaking amplitude 10 times larger than one that measures 4.0.
    a. Richter magnitude scale
    b. Medvedev-Sponheuer-Karnik scale
    c. Seismic scale
    d. China Seismic Intensity Scale

2. The lithosphere is broken up into what are called _____. In the case of Earth, there are eight major and many minor plates The lithospheric plates ride on the asthenosphere. These plates move in relation to one another at one of three types of plate boundaries: convergent, or collisional boundaries; divergent boundaries, also called spreading centers; and transform boundaries.
    a. Forearc
    b. Panthalassa
    c. Subduction
    d. Tectonic plates

3. In geology, a _____ is a place where the Earth's crust and lithosphere are being pulled apart and is an example of extensional tectonics.

    Typical _____ features are a central linear downdropped fault segment, called a graben, with parallel normal faulting and _____-flank uplifts on either side forming a _____ valley, where the _____ remains above sea level. The axis of the _____ area commonly contains volcanic rocks and active volcanism is a part of many, but not all active _____ systems.

    a. 1700 Cascadia earthquake
    b. 1703 Genroku earthquake
    c. 1509 Istanbul earthquake
    d. Rift

4. _____ is the stress applied to materials resulting in their compaction (decrease of volume.) When a material is subjected to _____, then this material is under compression. Usually, _____ applied to bars, columns, etc.
    a. 1700 Cascadia earthquake
    b. 1703 Genroku earthquake
    c. 1509 Istanbul earthquake
    d. Compressive stress

5. _____ is the movement of the Earth's continents relative to each other. The hypothesis that continents 'drift' was first put forward by Abraham Ortelius in 1596 and was fully developed by Alfred Wegener in 1912. However, it was not until the development of the theory of plate tectonics in the 1960s, that a sufficient geological explanation of that movement was found.
    a. Subduction
    b. Plate tectonics
    c. Thrust fault
    d. Continental drift

6. In materials science, _____ is a change in the shape or size of an object due to an applied force. This can be a result of tensile (pulling) forces, compressive (pushing) forces, shear, bending or torsion (twisting.) _____ is often described as strain.
    a. Deformation
    b. Combe
    c. Melange
    d. Platform

7. In geology, _____ is transported rock debris overlying the solid bedrock. The term is also sometimes refers to organic debris so-transported. In the largest sense, it refers to the material left behind by retreating continental glaciers.

a. Fulgurites
b. Drift
c. Duricrust
d. Gibraltar Arc

8. _____ circulation in its most general sense is the circulation of hot water; 'hydros' in the Greek meaning water and 'thermos' meaning heat. _____ circulation occurs most often in the vicinity of sources of heat within the Earth's crust. This generally occurs near volcanic activity, but can occur in the deep crust related to the intrusion of granite, or as the result of orogeny or metamorphism.
a. Hydrothermal
b. Stoping
c. Permineralization
d. Seafloor spreading

9. _____ describes the large scale motions of Earth's lithosphere. The theory encompasses the older concepts of continental drift, developed during the first decades of the 20th century by Alfred Wegener, and seafloor spreading, understood during the 1960s.

The outermost part of the Earth's interior is made up of two layers: the lithosphere and the asthenosphere.

a. Nappe
b. Plate tectonics
c. Tectonic plates
d. Continental collision

10. An axial stress is a normal stress produced when a force acts parallel to the major axis of a body, e.g. column axially loaded (Figure 1.) If the forces pull the body producing an elongation, the axial stress is termed _____. If on the other hand the forces push the body reducing its length, the axial stress is termed compressive stress.
a. Tensile stress
b. Thixotropy
c. Viscosity
d. Shear stress

11. The _____ is an informal name for the supereon comprising the eons of the geologic timescale that came before the current Phanerozoic eon. It spans from the formation of Earth around 4500 Mya (million years ago) to the evolution of abundant macroscopic hard-shelled animals, which marked the beginning of the Cambrian, the first period of the first era of the Phanerozoic eon, some 542 Mya. It is named after the Roman name for Wales - Cambria - where rocks from this age were first studied.
a. 1703 Genroku earthquake
b. 1700 Cascadia earthquake
c. 1509 Istanbul earthquake
d. Precambrian

12. The _____ is the mechanically weak ductily-deforming region of the upper mantle of the Earth. It lies below the lithosphere, at depths between 100 and 200 km (~ 62 and 124 miles) below the surface, but perhaps extending as deep as 400 km (~ 249 miles.)

The _____ is a portion of the upper mantle just below the lithosphere that is involved in plate movements and isostatic adjustments. In spite of its heat, pressures keep it plastic, and it has a relatively low density. Seismic waves pass relatively slowly through the _____, compared to the overlying lithospheric mantle, thus it has been called the low-velocity zone. This was the observation that originally alerted seismologists to its presence and gave some information about its physical properties, as the speed of seismic waves decreases with decreasing rigidity.

a. Asthenosphere
b. AASHTO Soil Classification System
c. AL 333
d. AL 129-1

13. The _____ is the rigid outermost shell of a rocky planet.

In the Earth, the _____ includes the crust and the uppermost mantle, which constitute the hard and rigid outer layer of the planet. The _____ is underlain by the asthenosphere, the weaker, hotter, and deeper part of the upper mantle.

a. Forearc
b. Gorda Ridge
c. Lithosphere
d. Subduction

14. The _____ is a classification used for most Western Hemisphere tropical cyclones that exceed the intensities of tropical depressions and tropical storms. The scale divides hurricanes into five categories distinguished by the intensities of their sustained winds. In order to be classified as a hurricane, a tropical cyclone must have maximum sustained winds of at least 74 mph (33 m/s; 64 kt; 119 km/h.)

a. 1509 Istanbul earthquake
b. Saffir-Simpson Hurricane Scale
c. 1700 Cascadia earthquake
d. 1703 Genroku earthquake

15. The _____ is an oceanic tectonic plate beneath the Pacific Ocean.

To the north the easterly side is a divergent boundary with the Explorer Plate, the Juan de Fuca Plate and the Gorda Plate forming respectively the Explorer Ridge, the Juan de Fuca Ridge and the Gorda Ridge. In the middle the easterly side is a transform boundary with the North American Plate along the San Andreas Fault and a boundary with the Cocos Plate.

a. New Hebrides Plate
b. Scotia Plate
c. Gorda Plate
d. Pacific Plate

16. A _____ zone or _____ area is the interface between land and a stream. Plant communities along the river margins are called _____ vegetation, characterized by hydrophilic plants. _____ zones are significant in ecology, environmental management, and civil engineering because of their role in soil conservation, their biodiversity, and the influence they have on aquatic ecosystems.

a. 1509 Istanbul earthquake
b. Riparian
c. 1703 Genroku earthquake
d. 1700 Cascadia earthquake

17. _____ is one of the three main rock types (the others being sedimentary and metamorphic rock.) _____ is formed by magma (molten rock) being cooled and becoming solid . They may form with or without crystallization, either below the surface as intrusive (plutonic) rocks or on the surface as extrusive (volcanic) rocks. They make up approximately 95% of the upper part of the Earth's crust, but their great abundance is hidden on the Earth's surface by a relatively thin but widespread layer of sedimentary and metamorphic rocks.

a. AL 129-1
b. AASHTO Soil Classification System
c. AL 333
d. Igneous rock

18. _____ is the study of the record of the Earth's magnetic field preserved in various magnetic minerals through time. The study of _____ has demonstrated that the Earth's magnetic field varies substantially in both orientation and intensity through time. <
   a. Lichenometry
   b. Radiometric dating
   c. Cenomanian
   d. Paleomagnetism

19. _____ occurs at mid-ocean ridges, where new oceanic crust is formed through volcanic activity and then gradually moves away from the ridge. _____ helps explain continental drift in the theory of plate tectonics.

Earlier theories (e.g., by Alfred Wegener) of continental drift were that continents 'plowed' through the sea. The idea that the seafloor itself moves (and carries the continents with it) as it expands from a central axis was proposed by Harry Hess from Princeton University in the 1960s. The theory is well-accepted now, and the phenomenon is known to be caused by convection currents in the plastic, very weak upper mantle, or asthenosphere.

   a. Hydrothermal
   b. Mid-ocean ridge
   c. Seafloor spreading
   d. Permineralization

20. The _____ is the epoch from 1.8 million to 11550 years BP covering the world's recent period of repeated glaciations. The _____ epoch follows the Pliocene epoch and is followed by the Holocene epoch. The _____ is the third epoch of the Neogene period or 6th epoch of the Cenozoic Era. The end of the _____ corresponds with the retreat of the last continental glacier. It also corresponds with the end of the Paleolithic age used in archaeology.
   a. Late Pleistocene
   b. Sicilian Stage
   c. Tyrrhenian
   d. Pleistocene

21. _____, also known as the Pleistocene glaciation, the current ice age or simply the ice age, refers to the period of the last few million years in which permanent ice sheets were established in Antarctica and perhaps Greenland, and fluctuating ice sheets have occurred elsewhere The major effects of the ice age were erosion and deposition of material over large parts of the continents, modification of river systems, creation of millions of lakes, changes in sea level, development of pluvial lakes far from the ice margins, isostatic adjustment of the crust, and abnormal winds. It affected oceans, flooding, and biological communities.
   a. Glacial period
   b. Bergschrund
   c. Wolstonian Stage
   d. Quaternary glaciation

22. _____ is the largest and best-known genus of the extinct order of seed ferns known as Glossopteridales (or in some cases as Arberiales or Dictyopteridiales.)

The Glossopteridales arose around the beginning of the Permian on the great southern continent of Gondwana. These plants went on to become the dominant elements of the southern flora through the rest of the Permian but disappeared in almost all places at the end of the Permian.

   a. 1509 Istanbul earthquake
   b. Pteridospermatophyta
   c. Petrified wood
   d. Glossopteris

Chapter 3. Plate Tectonics

23. The _____ is a mid-ocean ridge, a divergent tectonic plate boundary located along the floor of the Atlantic Ocean, and the longest mountain range in the world. It separates the Eurasian Plate and North American Plate in the North Atlantic, and the African Plate from the South American Plate in the South Atlantic. The MAR extends from a junction with the Gakkel Ridge (Mid-Arctic Ridge) northeast of Greenland southward to the Bouvet Triple Junction in the South Atlantic.
   a. 1700 Cascadia earthquake
   b. 1703 Genroku earthquake
   c. 1509 Istanbul earthquake
   d. Mid-Atlantic Ridge

24. A _____ or sandbar is a somewhat linear landform within or extending into a body of water, typically composed of sand, silt or small pebbles. A bar is characteristically long and narrow and develops where a stream or ocean current promotes deposition of granular material, resulting in localized shallowing of the water. Bars can appear in the sea, in a lake, or in a river.

The term _____ can be applied to larger geological units that form off a coastline as part of the process of coastal erosion. These include spits and baymouth bars that form across the front of embayments and rias. A tombolo is a bar that forms an isthmus between an island or offshore rock and a mainland shore.
   a. 1700 Cascadia earthquake
   b. 1703 Genroku earthquake
   c. 1509 Istanbul earthquake
   d. Shoal

25. _____ are the preserved remains or traces of animals, plants, and other organisms from the remote past. The totality of _____, both discovered and undiscovered, and their placement in fossiliferous rock formations and sedimentary layers (strata) is known as the fossil record. The study of _____ across geological time, how they were formed, and the evolutionary relationships between taxa (phylogeny) are some of the most important functions of the science of paleontology.
   a. 1700 Cascadia earthquake
   b. 1509 Istanbul earthquake
   c. 1703 Genroku earthquake
   d. Fossils

26. A _____ is a mountain rising from the ocean seafloor that does not reach to the water's surface (sea level), and thus is not an island. These are typically formed from extinct volcanoes, that rise abruptly and are usually found rising from a seafloor of 1,000-4,000 meters depth. They are defined by oceanographers as independent features that rise to at least 1,000 meters above the seafloor.
   a. 1700 Cascadia earthquake
   b. 1509 Istanbul earthquake
   c. 1703 Genroku earthquake
   d. Seamount

27. _____ is a gas consisting primarily of methane. It is found associated with fossil fuels, in coal beds, as methane clathrates, and is created by methanogenic organisms in marshes, bogs, and landfills. It is an important fuel source, a major feedstock for fertilizers, and a potent greenhouse gas.
   a. 1509 Istanbul earthquake
   b. Natural gas
   c. 1700 Cascadia earthquake
   d. 1703 Genroku earthquake

28. _____ was the supercontinent that is theorized to have existed during the Paleozoic and Mesozoic eras about 250 million years ago, before the component continents were separated into their current configuration.

The name was first used by the German originator of the continental drift theory, Alfred Wegener, in the 1920 edition of his book The Origin of Continents and Oceans, in which a postulated supercontinent _____ played a key role.

Chapter 3. Plate Tectonics   23

The single enormous ocean which surrounded Pangaea is known as Panthalassa.

   a. 1700 Cascadia earthquake
   c. Pangea

   b. 1703 Genroku earthquake
   d. 1509 Istanbul earthquake

29.   Volatile organic compounds (_____) are gases or vapours emitted by various solids or liquids, many of which have short- and long-term adverse health effects. Household products that emit _____ include paint, paint strippers, cleaning supplies, pesticides, glues and adhesives, building materials and furnishings. Consequently, concentrations of many _____ are higher indoors (up to ten times higher) than outdoors.
   a. VOCs
   c. 1703 Genroku earthquake

   b. 1700 Cascadia earthquake
   d. 1509 Istanbul earthquake

30.   A _____ or transform boundary is a fault which runs along the boundary of a tectonic plate. The relative motion of such plates is horizontal in either sinistral or dextral direction. Typically, some vertical motion may also exist, but the principal vectors in a _____ are oriented horizontally.
   a. Petermann Orogeny
   c. Tectonites

   b. Transform fault
   d. Molasse basin

31.   _____, originally Gondwanaland, is the name given to a southern precursor-supercontinent and then as a remnant separated from Laurasia 180-200 million years ago during the breakup of the Pangaea supercontinent that existed about 500 to 200 Ma ago into two large segments. While the corresponding northern hemisphere continent Laurasia moved further north, the nearly equal in area _____ included most of the landmasses in today's southern hemisphere, including Antarctica, South America, Africa, Madagascar, Australia-New Guinea, and New Zealand, as well as Arabia and the Indian subcontinent, which have now moved into the Northern Hemisphere.
   a. Laurasia
   c. 1700 Cascadia earthquake

   b. 1509 Istanbul earthquake
   d. Gondwana

32.   _____ was a supercontinent that most recently existed as a part of the split of the Pangaean supercontinent in the late Mesozoic era. It included most of the landmasses which make up today's continents of the northern hemisphere, chiefly Laurentia (the name given to the North American craton), Baltica, Siberia, Kazakhstania, and the North China and East China cratons.
   a. Rodinia
   c. 1700 Cascadia earthquake

   b. 1509 Istanbul earthquake
   d. Laurasia

33.   The _____ is a tectonic plate covering most of North America, Greenland and part of Siberia. It extends eastward to the Mid-Atlantic Ridge and westward to the Chersky Range in eastern Siberia. The plate includes both continental and oceanic crust. The interior of the main continental landmass includes an extensive granitic core called a craton. Along most of the edges of this craton are fragments of crustal material called terranes, accreted to the craton by tectonic actions over the long span of geologic time. It is believed that much of North America west of the Rockies is composed of such terranes.
   a. Somali Plate
   c. Futuna Plate

   b. Jan Mayen Plate
   d. North American Plate

34.   In plate tectonics, a _____ is an actively deforming region where two tectonic plates or fragments of lithosphere move toward one another and collide. As a result of pressure and friction and plate material melting in the mantle, earthquakes and volcanoes are common near convergent boundaries.

a. Convergent boundary
b. Copperbelt Province
c. Divergent boundary
d. Mirovia

35. An _____ is the result of a sudden release of energy in the Earth's crust that creates seismic waves. They are recorded with a seismometer or the related and mostly obsolete Richter magnitude, with a magnitude 3 or lower _____ being mostly imperceptible and magnitude 7 causing serious damage over large areas.
   a. AL 129-1
   b. AASHTO Soil Classification System
   c. AL 333
   d. Earthquake

36. In geology, a _____ or _____ line is a planar fracture in rock in which the rock on one side of the fracture has moved with respect to the rock on the other side. Large _____s within the Earth's crust are the result of differential or shear motion and active _____ zones are the causal locations of most earthquakes. Earthquakes are caused by energy release during rapid slippage along a _____.
   a. Tarn
   b. Stack
   c. Streak
   d. Fault

37. A _____, sometimes called a composite volcano, is a tall, conical volcano with many layers (strata) of hardened lava, tephra, and volcanic ash. They are characterized by a steep profile and periodic, explosive eruptions. The lava that flows from a _____ tends to be viscous; it cools and hardens before spreading far.
   a. Nevado Sajama
   b. Stratovolcano
   c. Mount Overlord
   d. Mount Baker

38. _____ are waves that travel through the Earth or other elastic body, for example as the result of an earthquake, explosion, or some other process that imparts forces to the body. _____ are also continually excited on Earth by the incessant pounding of ocean waves (referred to as the microseism) and the wind. _____ are studied by seismologists, and measured by a seismograph, which records the output of a seismometer, or geophone.
   a. Rayleigh waves
   b. Paleoliquefaction
   c. Harmonic tremor
   d. Seismic waves

39. In geology, _____ is the process that takes place at convergent boundaries by which one tectonic plate moves under another tectonic plate, sinking into the Earth's mantle, as the plates converge. A _____ zone is an area on Earth where two tectonic plates move towards one another and _____ occurs. Rates of _____ are typically measured in centimeters per year, with the average rate of convergence being approximately 2 to 8 centimeters per year (about the rate a fingernail grows.)
   a. Gorda Ridge
   b. Nappe
   c. Divergent boundary
   d. Subduction

40. A _____ is an opening in a planet's surface or crust, which allows hot, molten rock, ash, and gases to escape from below the surface. Volcanic activity involving the extrusion of rock tends to form mountains or features like mountains over a period of time.
   a. 1509 Istanbul earthquake
   b. 1700 Cascadia earthquake
   c. 1703 Genroku earthquake
   d. Volcano

Chapter 3. Plate Tectonics

41. _____, meaning 'new eruption', is a volcano located on the Alaska Peninsula in Katmai National Park and Preserve, about 290 miles (470 km) southwest of Anchorage. Formed in 1912 during one of the largest volcanic eruptions of the 20th century, _____ released 30 times the volume of magma as the 1980 eruption of Mount St. Helens. Map showing volcanoes of Alaska.

One of the largest eruptions of the 20th century occurred in 1912, from June 6 to June 8, to form _____.

- a. 1509 Istanbul earthquake
- b. 1703 Genroku earthquake
- c. 1700 Cascadia earthquake
- d. Novarupta

42. _____ is the removal of solids (sediment, soil, rock and other particles) in the natural environment. It usually occurs due to transport by wind, water, or ice; by down-slope creep of soil and other material under the force of gravity; or by living organisms, such as burrowing animals, in the case of bioerosion.

_____ is distinguished from weathering, which is the process of chemical or physical breakdown of the minerals in the rocks, although the two processes may occur concurrently.

- a. AL 333
- b. AASHTO Soil Classification System
- c. Erosion
- d. AL 129-1

43. _____ is a 2.4 mi^2 atoll located in the North Pacific Ocean (near the northwestern end of the Hawaiian archipelago), about one-third of the way between Honolulu and Tokyo.

_____ is part of a chain of volcanic islands, atolls, and seamounts extending from Hawai'i up to the tip of the Aleutian Islands and known as the Hawaii-Emperor chain. Midway was formed roughly 28 million years ago when the seabed underneath it was over the same hotspot from which the Island of Hawai'i is now being formed. In fact, Midway was once a shield volcano perhaps as large as the island of Lana'i.

- a. 1700 Cascadia earthquake
- b. 1509 Istanbul earthquake
- c. 1703 Genroku earthquake
- d. Midway Atoll

44. _____ is a geyser in Yellowstone National Park in the U.S. state of Wyoming.

The geyser is located on the Firehole River within the Upper Geyser Basin. The geyser shoots steam and water to heights of 75 feet (23 m) in an arch over the river.

- a. Riverside Geyser
- b. 1509 Istanbul earthquake
- c. 1700 Cascadia earthquake
- d. 1703 Genroku earthquake

45. A _____ is a phenomenon of fluid dynamics that occurs in situations where there are temperature differences within a body of liquid or gas.

Fluids are materials that exhibit the property of flow. Both gases and liquids have fluid properties, and in sufficient quantity, even particulate solids such as salt, grain, and gravel show some fluid properties. When a volume of fluid is heated, it expands and becomes less dense and thus more buoyant than the surrounding fluid. The colder, denser fluid settles underneath the warmer, less dense fluid and forces it to rise. Such movement is called convection, and the moving body of liquid is referred to as a _____.

- a. 1509 Istanbul earthquake
- b. 1700 Cascadia earthquake
- c. 1703 Genroku earthquake
- d. Convection cell

46. In geology, a _____ is a location on the Earth's surface that has experienced active volcanism for a long period of time.

J. Tuzo Wilson came up with the idea in 1963 that volcanic chains like the Hawaiian Islands result from the slow movement of a tectonic plate across a 'fixed' _____ deep beneath the surface of the planet.

- a. Hotspot
- b. 1509 Istanbul earthquake
- c. 1700 Cascadia earthquake
- d. 1703 Genroku earthquake

47. The _____ is a fundamental concept in geology that describes the dynamic transitions through geologic time among the three main rock types: sedimentary, metamorphic, and igneous. Each type of rock is altered or destroyed when it is forced out of its equilibrium conditions. An igneous rock such as basalt may break down and dissolve when exposed to the atmosphere, or melt as it is subducted under a continent.
- a. Metamorphic rock
- b. Metavolcanic rock
- c. Serpentinite
- d. Rock cycle

Chapter 4. Earthquakes

1. The _____ is a large enclosed plain, approximately 50 miles (80 km) long and up to 15 miles (24 km) across, in southeastern San Luis Obispo County, California, about 100 miles (160 km) northwest of Los Angeles, California. The most prevalent geologic feature of the _____s is the San Andreas Fault. It is a right lateral fault which runs along the northeast of the Plain, at the base of the Elkhorn Scarp, and forms the boundary between the Pacific and North American Plates. Although the fault runs through California all the way from Cape Mendocino to just south of Los Angeles, the _____ remains one of the best places to study it.
   a. Carrizo Plain
   b. 1509 Istanbul earthquake
   c. 1700 Cascadia earthquake
   d. 1703 Genroku earthquake

2. An _____ is the result of a sudden release of energy in the Earth's crust that creates seismic waves. They are recorded with a seismometer or the related and mostly obsolete Richter magnitude, with a magnitude 3 or lower _____ being mostly imperceptible and magnitude 7 causing serious damage over large areas.
   a. Earthquake
   b. AL 129-1
   c. AL 333
   d. AASHTO Soil Classification System

3. The _____ is a geologic fault zone capable of generating significantly destructive earthquakes. About 60 kilometers long, it lies mainly along the western base of the hills on the east side of San Francisco Bay. It runs through densely-populated areas, including the cities of Richmond, El Cerrito, Berkeley, Oakland, San Leandro, Hayward, Fremont, and San Jose.

The _____ is parallel to its more famous (and much longer) westerly neighbor, the San Andreas Fault, which lies offshore and through the San Francisco peninsula.

   a. 1509 Istanbul earthquake
   b. 1700 Cascadia earthquake
   c. Hayward Fault Zone
   d. 1703 Genroku earthquake

4. A _____ or sandbar is a somewhat linear landform within or extending into a body of water, typically composed of sand, silt or small pebbles. A bar is characteristically long and narrow and develops where a stream or ocean current promotes deposition of granular material, resulting in localized shallowing of the water. Bars can appear in the sea, in a lake, or in a river.

The term _____ can be applied to larger geological units that form off a coastline as part of the process of coastal erosion. These include spits and baymouth bars that form across the front of embayments and rias. A tombolo is a bar that forms an isthmus between an island or offshore rock and a mainland shore.

   a. 1509 Istanbul earthquake
   b. 1700 Cascadia earthquake
   c. 1703 Genroku earthquake
   d. Shoal

5. The _____ is an explanation for how energy is spread during earthquakes. As plates shift on opposite sides of a fault are subjected to force, they accumulate energy and slowly deform until their internal strength is exceeded. At that time, a sudden movement occurs along the fault, releasing the accumulated energy, and the rocks snap back to their original undeformed shape.
   a. Elastic rebound theory
   b. East Pacific Rise
   c. Azores-Gibraltar Transform Fault
   d. Obduction

6. The _____ or epicentre is the point on the Earth's surface that is directly above the hypocenter or focus, the point where an earthquake or underground explosion originates.

The _____ is usually the location of greatest damage. However, in some cases the _____ is above the start of a much larger event.

   a. AL 333
   c. AASHTO Soil Classification System
   b. AL 129-1
   d. Epicenter

7. In geology, a _____ or _____ line is a planar fracture in rock in which the rock on one side of the fracture has moved with respect to the rock on the other side. Large _____s within the Earth's crust are the result of differential or shear motion and active _____ zones are the causal locations of most earthquakes. Earthquakes are caused by energy release during rapid slippage along a _____.
   a. Fault
   c. Streak
   b. Stack
   d. Tarn

8. _____ circulation in its most general sense is the circulation of hot water; 'hydros' in the Greek meaning water and 'thermos' meaning heat. _____ circulation occurs most often in the vicinity of sources of heat within the Earth's crust. This generally occurs near volcanic activity, but can occur in the deep crust related to the intrusion of granite, or as the result of orogeny or metamorphism.
   a. Stoping
   c. Permineralization
   b. Seafloor spreading
   d. Hydrothermal

9. The _____, refers to the site of an earthquake or to that of a nuclear explosion. In the former, it is a synonym of the focus; in the latter, of ground zero.

The location of an earthquake's _____ is the position where the energy stored in the strain in the rock is released, which occurs at the focal depth below the epicentre. The focal depth can be calculated from measurements based on seismic wave phenomena.

   a. Hypocenter
   c. Maximum magnitude
   b. Harmonic tremor
   d. Seismic gap

10. A _____ is a mountain rising from the ocean seafloor that does not reach to the water's surface (sea level), and thus is not an island. These are typically formed from extinct volcanoes, that rise abruptly and are usually found rising from a seafloor of 1,000-4,000 meters depth. They are defined by oceanographers as independent features that rise to at least 1,000 meters above the seafloor.
   a. Seamount
   c. 1700 Cascadia earthquake
   b. 1703 Genroku earthquake
   d. 1509 Istanbul earthquake

11. _____ are type of elastic wave, also called seismic waves, that can travel through gases, elastic solids and liquids, including the Earth. _____ can be produced by earthquakes and recorded by seismometers.
   a. 1703 Genroku earthquake
   c. 1700 Cascadia earthquake
   b. 1509 Istanbul earthquake
   d. P-waves

12. A type of seismic wave, the _____, secondary wave or shear wave (sometimes called an elastic _____) is one of the two main types of elastic body waves, so named because they move through the body of an object, unlike surface waves.

Chapter 4. Earthquakes 29

The _____ move as a shear or transverse wave, so motion is perpendicular to the direction of wave propagation: _____s, like waves in a rope, as opposed to waves moving through a slinky, the P-wave. The wave moves through elastic media, and the main restoring force comes from shear effects.

- a. 1703 Genroku earthquake
- b. 1700 Cascadia earthquake
- c. 1509 Istanbul earthquake
- d. S-wave

13. _____ are waves that travel through the Earth or other elastic body, for example as the result of an earthquake, explosion, or some other process that imparts forces to the body. _____ are also continually excited on Earth by the incessant pounding of ocean waves (referred to as the microseism) and the wind. _____ are studied by seismologists, and measured by a seismograph, which records the output of a seismometer, or geophone.
- a. Seismic waves
- b. Paleoliquefaction
- c. Harmonic tremor
- d. Rayleigh waves

14. Study of geological _____ is related to the study of structural geology, rock microstructure or rock texture and fault mechanics.

_____ is the response of a rock to deformation usually by compressive stress and forms particular textures. _____ can be homogeneous or non-homogeneous, and may be pure _____ or simple _____.

- a. Michoud fault
- b. Transform fault
- c. Graben
- d. Shear

15. In physics, a _____ is a mechanical wave that propagates along the interface between differing media, usually two fluids with different densities. A _____ can also be an electromagnetic wave guided by a refractive index gradient. In radio transmission, a ground wave is a _____ that propagates close to the surface of the Earth.
- a. 1700 Cascadia earthquake
- b. 1509 Istanbul earthquake
- c. 1703 Genroku earthquake
- d. Surface wave

16. The _____ is an informal name for the supereon comprising the eons of the geologic timescale that came before the current Phanerozoic eon. It spans from the formation of Earth around 4500 Mya (million years ago) to the evolution of abundant macroscopic hard-shelled animals, which marked the beginning of the Cambrian, the first period of the first era of the Phanerozoic eon, some 542 Mya. It is named after the Roman name for Wales - Cambria - where rocks from this age were first studied.
- a. 1703 Genroku earthquake
- b. 1509 Istanbul earthquake
- c. 1700 Cascadia earthquake
- d. Precambrian

17. The _____, also known as the local magnitude (M_L) scale, assigns a single number to quantify the amount of seismic energy released by an earthquake. It is a base-10 logarithmic scale obtained by calculating the logarithm of the combined horizontal amplitude of the largest displacement from zero on a Wood-Anderson torsion seismometer output. So, for example, an earthquake that measures 5.0 on the Richter scale has a shaking amplitude 10 times larger than one that measures 4.0.
- a. China Seismic Intensity Scale
- b. Medvedev-Sponheuer-Karnik scale
- c. Seismic scale
- d. Richter magnitude scale

Chapter 4. Earthquakes

18. The _____ characterizes the scratch resistance of various minerals through the ability of a harder material to scratch a softer material. It was created in 1812 by the German mineralogist Friedrich Mohs and is one of several definitions of hardness in materials science. The method, however, is of great antiquity, having first been mentioned by Theophrastus in his treatise On Stones in ca 300 BC, followed by Pliny the Elder in his Naturalis Historia circa A.D.
    a. 1703 Genroku earthquake
    b. Mohs scale of mineral hardness
    c. 1509 Istanbul earthquake
    d. 1700 Cascadia earthquake

19. The _____ is used by seismologists to measure the size of earthquakes in terms of the energy released. The magnitude is based on the moment of the earthquake, which is equal to the rigidity of the Earth multiplied by the average amount of slip on the fault and the size of the area that slipped. The scale was developed in the 1970s to succeed the 1930s-era Richter magnitude scale, M_L.
    a. Surface wave magnitude
    b. Mercalli intensity scale
    c. Seismic scale
    d. Moment magnitude scale

20. A _____ is an opening in a planet's surface or crust, which allows hot, molten rock, ash, and gases to escape from below the surface. Volcanic activity involving the extrusion of rock tends to form mountains or features like mountains over a period of time.
    a. 1700 Cascadia earthquake
    b. 1509 Istanbul earthquake
    c. 1703 Genroku earthquake
    d. Volcano

21. An _____ is an earthquake that occurs after a previous earthquake (the main shock.) An _____ is in the same region of the main shock but is always of smaller magnitude strength. If an _____ is larger than the main shock, the _____ is redesignated as the main shock and the original main shock is redesignated as a foreshock.
    a. AL 129-1
    b. AL 333
    c. AASHTO Soil Classification System
    d. Aftershock

22. _____ is the movement of the Earth's continents relative to each other. The hypothesis that continents 'drift' was first put forward by Abraham Ortelius in 1596 and was fully developed by Alfred Wegener in 1912. However, it was not until the development of the theory of plate tectonics in the 1960s, that a sufficient geological explanation of that movement was found.
    a. Thrust fault
    b. Subduction
    c. Plate tectonics
    d. Continental drift

23. In geology, _____ is transported rock debris overlying the solid bedrock. The term is also sometimes refers to organic debris so-transported. In the largest sense, it refers to the material left behind by retreating continental glaciers.
    a. Gibraltar Arc
    b. Fulgurites
    c. Duricrust
    d. Drift

24. _____ is the geomorphic process by which soil, regolith, and rock move downslope under the force of gravity. Types of _____ include creep, slides, flows, topples, and falls, each with its own characteristic features, and taking place over timescales from seconds to years. _____ occurs on both terrestrial and submarine slopes, and has been observed on Earth, Mars, and Venus.
    a. 1700 Cascadia earthquake
    b. Soil liquefaction
    c. 1509 Istanbul earthquake
    d. Mass wasting

25. _____ is a naturally occurring granular material composed of finely divided rock and mineral particles.

Chapter 4. Earthquakes

As the term is used by geologists, _____ particles range in diameter from 0.0625 (or $>^1>/_{16}$ mm, or 62.5 micrometers) to 2 millimeters. An individual particle in this range size is termed a _____ grain.

a. 1703 Genroku earthquake
b. 1509 Istanbul earthquake
c. 1700 Cascadia earthquake
d. Sand

26. _____ is the largest volcano on earth in terms of area covered and one of five volcanoes that form the Island of Hawaii in the U.S. state of Hawaiʻi in the Pacific Ocean. It is an active shield volcano, with a volume estimated at approximately 18,000 cubic miles (75,000 kmÂ³), although its peak is about 120 feet (37 m) lower than that of its neighbor, Mauna Kea. The Hawaiian name '_____' means 'Long Mountain'.

a. 1703 Genroku earthquake
b. 1509 Istanbul earthquake
c. Mauna Loa
d. 1700 Cascadia earthquake

27. _____ crater is a crater on Mars's moon Deimos. It is about 3km in diameter. _____ crater is named after Jonathan _____, who predicted the existence of the moons of Mars.

a. 1700 Cascadia earthquake
b. 1703 Genroku earthquake
c. 1509 Istanbul earthquake
d. Swift

28. A _____ is a segment of an active fault that has not slipped in an unusually long time when compared with other segments along the same structure. _____ hypothesis/theory states that, over long periods of time, the displacement on any segment must be equal to that experienced by all the other parts of the fault. Any large and longstanding gap is therefore considered to be the fault segment most likely to suffer future earthquakes.

a. Seismic gap
b. Strong ground motion
c. Hypocenter
d. Seismic shadowing

29. _____ is the naturally occurring, unconsolidated or loose covering on the Earth's surface. _____ is composed of particles of broken rock that have been altered by chemical, biological and environmental processes including weathering and erosion. _____ is different from its parent rock(s) source(s), altered by interactions between the lithosphere, hydrosphere, atmosphere, and the biosphere.

a. Slump
b. 1509 Istanbul earthquake
c. Topsoil
d. Soil

30. The _____ is a continental tectonic plate consisting primarily of the country of Turkey.

The easterly side is a boundary with the Arabian Plate, the East Anatolian Fault, a left lateral transform fault.

The southerly and southwesterly sides comprise a convergent boundary with the African Plate, manifest in compressive features of the oceanic crust beneath the Mediterranean as well as within the continental crust of Anatolia itself, and also by what are generally considered to be subduction zones along the Hellenic and Cyprus Arcs.

a. AASHTO Soil Classification System
b. AL 129-1
c. Anatolian plate
d. AL 333

31. The _____ is a major seismic zone in the Southern and Midwestern United States stretching to the southwest from New Madrid, Missouri.

The New Madrid fault system was responsible for the 1812 New Madrid Earthquake and has the potential to produce damaging earthquakes on an average of every 300 to 500 years. Since 1812 frequent smaller intraplate earthquakes were recorded for the area.

The _____ is made up of reactivated faults that formed when North America began to split or rift apart during the breakup of the supercontinent Rodinia in the Neoproterozoic Era (about 750 million years ago). The resulting rift system failed but remained as an aulacogen (a scar or zone of weakness).

- a. New Madrid Seismic Zone
- b. 1700 Cascadia earthquake
- c. 1703 Genroku earthquake
- d. 1509 Istanbul earthquake

32. _____ uses the results of a seismic hazard analysis, and includes both consequence and probability. _____ has been defined, for most management purposes, as the potential economic, social and environmental consequences of hazardous events that may occur in a specified period of time. A building located in a region of high seismic hazard is at lower risk if it is built to sound seismic engineering principles.

- a. Seismic microzonation
- b. Seismic risk
- c. 1509 Istanbul earthquake
- d. 1700 Cascadia earthquake

Chapter 5. Volcanoes

1. _____ is a geyser in Yellowstone National Park in the U.S. state of Wyoming.

The geyser is located on the Firehole River within the Upper Geyser Basin. The geyser shoots steam and water to heights of 75 feet (23 m) in an arch over the river.

   a. 1509 Istanbul earthquake
   c. 1703 Genroku earthquake
   b. Riverside Geyser
   d. 1700 Cascadia earthquake

2. Volatile organic compounds (_____) are gases or vapours emitted by various solids or liquids, many of which have short- and long-term adverse health effects. Household products that emit _____ include paint, paint strippers, cleaning supplies, pesticides, glues and adhesives, building materials and furnishings. Consequently, concentrations of many _____ are higher indoors (up to ten times higher) than outdoors.
   a. 1509 Istanbul earthquake
   c. 1703 Genroku earthquake
   b. 1700 Cascadia earthquake
   d. VOCs

3. A _____ is an opening in a planet's surface or crust, which allows hot, molten rock, ash, and gases to escape from below the surface. Volcanic activity involving the extrusion of rock tends to form mountains or features like mountains over a period of time.
   a. 1700 Cascadia earthquake
   c. 1703 Genroku earthquake
   b. 1509 Istanbul earthquake
   d. Volcano

4. The _____ is a continental tectonic plate consisting primarily of the country of Turkey.

The easterly side is a boundary with the Arabian Plate, the East Anatolian Fault, a left lateral transform fault.

The southerly and southwesterly sides comprise a convergent boundary with the African Plate, manifest in compressive features of the oceanic crust beneath the Mediterranean as well as within the continental crust of Anatolia itself, and also by what are generally considered to be subduction zones along the Hellenic and Cyprus Arcs.

   a. Anatolian plate
   c. AL 129-1
   b. AASHTO Soil Classification System
   d. AL 333

5. A _____ is a mountain rising from the ocean seafloor that does not reach to the water's surface (sea level), and thus is not an island. These are typically formed from extinct volcanoes, that rise abruptly and are usually found rising from a seafloor of 1,000-4,000 meters depth. They are defined by oceanographers as independent features that rise to at least 1,000 meters above the seafloor.
   a. 1703 Genroku earthquake
   c. 1700 Cascadia earthquake
   b. 1509 Istanbul earthquake
   d. Seamount

6. _____ is an igneous, volcanic rock, of intermediate composition, with aphanitic to porphyritic texture. The mineral assemblage is typically dominated by plagioclase plus pyroxene and/or hornblende. Magnetite, zircon, apatite, ilmenite, biotite, and garnet are common accessory minerals.
   a. Andesite
   c. AL 129-1
   b. AASHTO Soil Classification System
   d. AL 333

Chapter 5. Volcanoes

7. In geology, a _____ or _____ line is a planar fracture in rock in which the rock on one side of the fracture has moved with respect to the rock on the other side. Large _____s within the Earth's crust are the result of differential or shear motion and active _____ zones are the causal locations of most earthquakes. Earthquakes are caused by energy release during rapid slippage along a _____.
   a. Fault
   c. Streak
   b. Stack
   d. Tarn

8. _____ is a term used in geology to refer to silicate minerals, magma, and rocks which are enriched in the lighter elements such as silicon, oxygen, aluminium, sodium, and potassium. _____ minerals are usually light in color and have specific gravities less than 3. Common _____ minerals include quartz, muscovite, orthoclase, and the sodium-rich plagioclase feldspars.
   a. Metamorphic zone
   c. Tephra
   b. Rock cycle
   d. Felsic

9. _____ is an adjective describing a silicate mineral or rock that is rich in magnesium and iron; the term was derived by contracting 'magnesium' and 'ferric'. Most _____ minerals are dark in color and the specific gravity is greater than 3. Common rock-forming _____ minerals include olivine, pyroxene, amphibole, and biotite.

   _____ lava, before cooling, has a low viscosity, in comparison to felsic lava, due to the lower silica content in _____ magma. Water and other volatiles can more easily and gradually escape from _____ lava, so eruptions of volcanoes made of _____ lavas are less explosively violent than felsic lava eruptions.

   a. 1509 Istanbul earthquake
   c. Mafic
   b. 1703 Genroku earthquake
   d. 1700 Cascadia earthquake

10. _____ is molten rock that is found beneath the surface of the Earth, and may also exist on other terrestrial planets. Besides molten rock, _____ may also contain suspended crystals and gas bubbles. _____ often collects in a _____ chamber inside a volcano. _____ is capable of intrusion into adjacent rocks, extrusion onto the surface as lava, and explosive ejection as tephra to form pyroclastic rock.
   a. Laccolith
   c. Magma
   b. Pluton
   d. Volcanic rock

11. _____ is an igneous, volcanic (extrusive) rock, of felsic (silicon-rich) composition. It may have any texture from aphanitic to porphyritic. The mineral assemblage is usually quartz, alkali feldspar and plagioclase. Biotite and hornblende are common accessory minerals.

   _____ can be considered as the extrusive equivalent to the plutonic granite rock, and consequently, outcroppings of it often bear a resemblance to granite. Due to their high content of silica and low iron and magnesium contents, _____ melts are highly polymerized and form highly viscous lavas.

   a. 1703 Genroku earthquake
   c. 1509 Istanbul earthquake
   b. Rhyolite
   d. 1700 Cascadia earthquake

12. In geology, a _____ is a place where the Earth's crust and lithosphere are being pulled apart and is an example of extensional tectonics.

Typical _____ features are a central linear downdropped fault segment, called a graben, with parallel normal faulting and _____-flank uplifts on either side forming a _____ valley, where the _____ remains above sea level. The axis of the _____ area commonly contains volcanic rocks and active volcanism is a part of many, but not all active _____ systems.

a. 1700 Cascadia earthquake
b. 1509 Istanbul earthquake
c. 1703 Genroku earthquake
d. Rift

13. The chemical compound silicon dioxide, also known as _____ , is an oxide of silicon with a chemical formula of SiO_2 and has been known for its hardness since antiquity. _____ is most commonly found in nature as sand or quartz, as well as in the cell walls of diatoms. It is a principal component of most types of glass and substances such as concrete.

a. 1700 Cascadia earthquake
b. 1509 Istanbul earthquake
c. 1703 Genroku earthquake
d. Silica

14. The _____ is an area where large numbers of earthquakes and volcanic eruptions occur in the basin of the Pacific Ocean. In a 40,000 km horseshoe shape, it is associated with a nearly continuous series of oceanic trenches, volcanic arcs, and volcanic belts and/or plate movements. The _____ has 452 volcanoes and is home to over 75% of the world's active and dormant volcanoes.

a. 1703 Genroku earthquake
b. 1509 Istanbul earthquake
c. 1700 Cascadia earthquake
d. Pacific Ring of Fire

15. In geology, a _____ is a location on the Earth's surface that has experienced active volcanism for a long period of time.

J. Tuzo Wilson came up with the idea in 1963 that volcanic chains like the Hawaiian Islands result from the slow movement of a tectonic plate across a 'fixed' _____ deep beneath the surface of the planet.

a. 1509 Istanbul earthquake
b. 1700 Cascadia earthquake
c. Hotspot
d. 1703 Genroku earthquake

16. _____ occurs at mid-ocean ridges, where new oceanic crust is formed through volcanic activity and then gradually moves away from the ridge. _____ helps explain continental drift in the theory of plate tectonics.

Earlier theories (e.g., by Alfred Wegener) of continental drift were that continents 'plowed' through the sea. The idea that the seafloor itself moves (and carries the continents with it) as it expands from a central axis was proposed by Harry Hess from Princeton University in the 1960s. The theory is well-accepted now, and the phenomenon is known to be caused by convection currents in the plastic, very weak upper mantle, or asthenosphere.

a. Permineralization
b. Hydrothermal
c. Mid-ocean ridge
d. Seafloor spreading

Chapter 5. Volcanoes

17. _____ is the largest volcano on earth in terms of area covered and one of five volcanoes that form the Island of Hawaii in the U.S. state of Hawai>Ê»i in the Pacific Ocean. It is an active shield volcano, with a volume estimated at approximately 18,000 cubic miles (75,000 kmÂ³), although its peak is about 120 feet (37 m) lower than that of its neighbor, Mauna Kea. The Hawaiian name '_____' means 'Long Mountain'.
  a. 1509 Istanbul earthquake
  b. Mauna Loa
  c. 1703 Genroku earthquake
  d. 1700 Cascadia earthquake

18. _____, meaning 'new eruption', is a volcano located on the Alaska Peninsula in Katmai National Park and Preserve, about 290 miles (470 km) southwest of Anchorage. Formed in 1912 during one of the largest volcanic eruptions of the 20th century, _____ released 30 times the volume of magma as the 1980 eruption of Mount St. Helens. Map showing volcanoes of Alaska.

One of the largest eruptions of the 20th century occurred in 1912, from June 6 to June 8, to form _____.

  a. 1703 Genroku earthquake
  b. 1700 Cascadia earthquake
  c. 1509 Istanbul earthquake
  d. Novarupta

19. _____ is a common extrusive volcanic rock. It is usually grey to black and fine-grained due to rapid cooling of lava at the surface of a planet. It may be porphyritic containing larger crystals in a fine matrix, or vesicular, or frothy scoria.
  a. 1700 Cascadia earthquake
  b. 1703 Genroku earthquake
  c. 1509 Istanbul earthquake
  d. Basalt

20. A _____, sometimes called a composite volcano, is a tall, conical volcano with many layers (strata) of hardened lava, tephra, and volcanic ash. They are characterized by a steep profile and periodic, explosive eruptions. The lava that flows from a _____ tends to be viscous; it cools and hardens before spreading far.
  a. Mount Overlord
  b. Nevado Sajama
  c. Mount Baker
  d. Stratovolcano

21. A _____ or trap basalt is the result of a giant volcanic eruption or series of eruptions that coats large stretches of land or the ocean floor with basalt lava. _____s have occurred on continental scales (large igneous provinces) in prehistory, creating great plateaus and mountain ranges. _____s have erupted at random intervals throughout geological history and are clear evidence that the Earth undergoes periods of enhanced activity rather than being in a uniform steady state.
  a. Charnockite
  b. Welded tuff
  c. Flood basalt
  d. Tuff

22. _____ are waves that travel through the Earth or other elastic body, for example as the result of an earthquake, explosion, or some other process that imparts forces to the body. _____ are also continually excited on Earth by the incessant pounding of ocean waves (referred to as the microseism) and the wind. _____ are studied by seismologists, and measured by a seismograph, which records the output of a seismometer, or geophone.
  a. Paleoliquefaction
  b. Seismic waves
  c. Harmonic tremor
  d. Rayleigh waves

23. Study of geological _____ is related to the study of structural geology, rock microstructure or rock texture and fault mechanics.

Chapter 5. Volcanoes

_____ is the response of a rock to deformation usually by compressive stress and forms particular textures. _____ can be homogeneous or non-homogeneous, and may be pure _____ or simple _____.

a. Shear
c. Graben

b. Michoud fault
d. Transform fault

24. A _____ is generally a large area of exposed Precambrian crystalline igneous and high-grade metamorphic rocks that form tectonically stable areas. In all cases, the age of these rocks is greater than 570 million years and sometimes dates back 2 to 3.5 billion years. They have been little affected by tectonic events following the end of the Precambrian Era, and are relatively flat regions where mountain building, faulting, and other tectonic processes are greatly diminished compared with the activity that occurs at the margins of the _____s and the boundaries between tectonic plates.

a. Shield
c. 1703 Genroku earthquake

b. 1509 Istanbul earthquake
d. 1700 Cascadia earthquake

25. A _____ is a large volcano with shallow-sloping sides.

They are formed by lava flows of low viscosity - lava that flows easily. Consequently, a volcanic mountain having a broad profile is built up over time by flow after flow of relatively fluid basaltic lava issuing from vents or fissures on the surface of the volcano

a. 1700 Cascadia earthquake
c. 1703 Genroku earthquake

b. 1509 Istanbul earthquake
d. Shield volcano

26. _____ are type of elastic wave, also called seismic waves, that can travel through gases, elastic solids and liquids, including the Earth. _____ can be produced by earthquakes and recorded by seismometers.

a. 1509 Istanbul earthquake
c. 1703 Genroku earthquake

b. 1700 Cascadia earthquake
d. P-waves

27. A _____ is a pyroclastic material. They are extrusive igneous rocks, and are similar to pumice, which has so many cavities and is such low-density that it can float on water.

a. Pit crater
c. Cinder

b. Volcanic ash
d. Supervolcano

28. A _____ or scoria cone is a steep conical hill of volcanic fragments that accumulate around and downwind from a volcanic vent. The rock fragments, often called cinders or scoria, are glassy and contain numerous gas bubbles 'frozen' into place as magma exploded into the air and then cooled quickly. _____s range in size from tens to hundreds of meters tall.

a. 1703 Genroku earthquake
c. 1509 Istanbul earthquake

b. Cinder cone
d. 1700 Cascadia earthquake

Chapter 5. Volcanoes

29. _____ are clastic rocks composed solely or primarily of volcanic materials. Where the volcanic material has been transported and reworked through mechanical action, such as by wind or water, these rocks are termed volcaniclastic. Commonly associated with explosive volcanic activity - such as Plinian or krakatoan eruption styles, or phreatomagmatic eruptions - pyroclastic deposits are commonly formed from airborne ash, lapilli and bombs or blocks ejected from the volcano itself, mixed in with shattered country rock.

   a. Welded tuff
   b. Tuff
   c. Scoria
   d. Pyroclastic rocks

30. _____ is a dormant volcano in the U.S. state of Hawaii, one of five volcanoes which together form the island of Hawaii. _____ means 'white mountain' in the Hawaiian language, a reference to its summit being regularly covered by snow in winter.

The peak of _____ is 13,803 feet (4,207 m) above mean sea level but 33,476 feet (10,203 m) above its base on the floor of the Pacific Ocean.

   a. 1509 Istanbul earthquake
   b. 1703 Genroku earthquake
   c. 1700 Cascadia earthquake
   d. Mauna Kea

31. _____ was a supercontinent that most recently existed as a part of the split of the Pangaean supercontinent in the late Mesozoic era. It included most of the landmasses which make up today's continents of the northern hemisphere, chiefly Laurentia (the name given to the North American craton), Baltica, Siberia, Kazakhstania, and the North China and East China cratons.

   a. 1509 Istanbul earthquake
   b. Rodinia
   c. 1700 Cascadia earthquake
   d. Laurasia

32. In geology, _____ refers to heat sources within the planet. _____ is technically an adjective (e.g., _____ energy) but in U.S. English the word has attained frequent use as a noun .

The planet's internal heat was originally generated during its accretion, due to gravitational binding energy, and since then additional heat has continued to be generated by decay heat from the radioactive decay of elements.

   a. Fault
   b. Diamond Head
   c. Platform
   d. Geothermal

33. _____ is power extracted from heat stored in the earth. This geothermal energy originates from the original formation of the planet, from radioactive decay of minerals, and from solar energy absorbed at the surface. It has been used for space heating and bathing since ancient roman times, but is now better known for generating electricity.

   a. Geothermal desalination
   b. Hot Dry Rock Geothermal Energy
   c. Geothermal gradient
   d. Geothermal power

34. _____ is molten rock expelled by a volcano during eruption. When first expelled from a volcanic vent, it is a liquid at temperatures from 700 >°C to 1,200 >°C (1,300 >°F to 2,200 >°F.) Although _____ is quite viscous, with about 100,000 times the viscosity of water, it can flow great distances before cooling and solidifying, because of both its thixotropic and shear thinning properties.

Chapter 5. Volcanoes

a. Lapilli
b. Pit crater
c. Cinder
d. Lava

35. The _____ is a mid-ocean ridge, a divergent tectonic plate boundary located along the floor of the Atlantic Ocean, and the longest mountain range in the world. It separates the Eurasian Plate and North American Plate in the North Atlantic, and the African Plate from the South American Plate in the South Atlantic. The MAR extends from a junction with the Gakkel Ridge (Mid-Arctic Ridge) northeast of Greenland southward to the Bouvet Triple Junction in the South Atlantic.
  a. 1700 Cascadia earthquake
  b. 1703 Genroku earthquake
  c. 1509 Istanbul earthquake
  d. Mid-Atlantic Ridge

36. A _____ is a type of mudflow or landslide composed of pyroclastic material and water that flows down from a volcano, typically along a river valley. The term '_____' originated in the Javanese language of Indonesia. They can be best described as volcanic mudflows. They may not necessarily be caused by volcanic activity, but at the very least do originate from some type of volcanism.
  a. Lahar
  b. 1509 Istanbul earthquake
  c. 1703 Genroku earthquake
  d. 1700 Cascadia earthquake

37. A _____ is a common and devastating result of some explosive volcanic eruptions. The flows are fast-moving currents of hot gas and rock (collectively known as tephra), which travel away from the volcano at speeds generally as great as 700 km/hr (450 mi/h.) The gas can reach temperatures of about 1,000 >°C (1,830 >°F). The flows normally hug the ground and travel downhill, or spread laterally under gravity. Their speed depends upon the density of the current, the volcanic output rate, and the gradient of the slope.
  a. Wadati-Benioff zone
  b. Cinder
  c. Volcanic gases
  d. Pyroclastic flow

38. _____ is a large 13 kilometres wide caldera situated to the west of Naples, Italy declared regional park in 2003. Today mostly lying underwater, the area comprises 24 craters and volcanic edifices, some of which present hydrothermal activity at Lucrino, Agnano and the town of Pozzuoli and effusive gaseous manifestations like the Solfatara crater, mythological home of the Roman god of fire, Vulcan. The area also features bradyseismic phenomena, which are most evident at the temple of Serapis in Pozzuoli.
  a. 1509 Istanbul earthquake
  b. 1700 Cascadia earthquake
  c. 1703 Genroku earthquake
  d. Campi Flegrei

39. _____ is a branch of atmospheric science in which the chemistry of the Earth's atmosphere and that of other planets is studied. It is a multidisciplinary field of research and draws on environmental chemistry, physics, meteorology, computer modeling, oceanography, geology and volcanology and other disciplines. Research is increasingly connected with other areas of study such as climatology.
  a. AASHTO Soil Classification System
  b. AL 129-1
  c. Atmospheric oxygenation event
  d. Atmospheric chemistry

40. A _____ occurs when rising magma makes contact with ground or surface water. The extreme temperature of the magma) causes near-instantaneous evaporation to steam resulting in an explosion of steam, water, ash, rock, and volcanic bombs. At Mount St. Helens hundreds of steam explosions preceded a 1980 plinian eruption of the volcano.
  a. Limnic eruption
  b. 1509 Istanbul earthquake
  c. Phreatomagmatic eruptions
  d. Phreatic eruption

Chapter 5. Volcanoes

41. _____ include a variety of substances given off by active (or, at times, by dormant) volcanoes. These include gases trapped in cavities (vesicles) in volcanic rocks, dissolved or dissociated gases in magma and lava, or gases emanating directly from lava or indirectly through ground water heated by volcanic action.

The sources of _____ on Earth include:

- primordial and recycled constituents from the Earth's mantle,
- assimilated constituents from the Earth's crust,
- groundwater and the Earth's atmosphere.

Substances that may become gaseous or give off gases when heated are termed volatile substances.

Gases are released from magma through volatile constituents reaching such high concentrations in the base magma that they evaporate.

    a. Pit crater   b. Volcanic gases
    c. Cinder   d. Pyroclastic flow

42. The _____ Era is one of three geologic eras of the Phanerozoic eon. The division of time into eras dates back to Giovanni Arduino, in the 18th century, although his original name for the era now called the '_____' was 'Secondary' (making the modern era the 'Tertiary'.)

The _____ was a time of tectonic, climatic and evolutionary activity. The continents gradually shifted from a state of connectedness into their present configuration; the drifting provided for speciation and other important evolutionary developments.

    a. 1703 Genroku earthquake   b. 1509 Istanbul earthquake
    c. 1700 Cascadia earthquake   d. Mesozoic

43. _____ circulation in its most general sense is the circulation of hot water; 'hydros' in the Greek meaning water and 'thermos' meaning heat. _____ circulation occurs most often in the vicinity of sources of heat within the Earth's crust. This generally occurs near volcanic activity, but can occur in the deep crust related to the intrusion of granite, or as the result of orogeny or metamorphism.

    a. Permineralization   b. Seafloor spreading
    c. Stoping   d. Hydrothermal

44. _____ is the chemical compound with the formula SO_2. It is produced by volcanoes and in various industrial processes. Since coal and petroleum often contain sulfur compounds, their combustion generates _____.

    a. 1700 Cascadia earthquake   b. 1703 Genroku earthquake
    c. 1509 Istanbul earthquake   d. Sulfur dioxide

45. An _____ is the result of a sudden release of energy in the Earth's crust that creates seismic waves. They are recorded with a seismometer or the related and mostly obsolete Richter magnitude, with a magnitude 3 or lower _____ being mostly imperceptible and magnitude 7 causing serious damage over large areas.

Chapter 5. Volcanoes

a. AL 333
b. AL 129-1
c. AASHTO Soil Classification System
d. Earthquake

46. _____ is a depression in eastern California that is adjacent to Mammoth Mountain. The valley is one of the largest calderas on earth, measuring about 32 kilometres (20 mi) long (east-west) and 17 kilometres (11 mi) wide (north-south.) The elevation of the floor of the caldera is 6,500 feet (2,000 m) in the east and 8,500 feet (2,600 m) in the west.
a. 1700 Cascadia earthquake
b. 1509 Istanbul earthquake
c. 1703 Genroku earthquake
d. Long Valley caldera

47. The _____ is the volcanic caldera in Yellowstone National Park in the United States. The caldera is located in the northwest corner of Wyoming, in which the vast majority of the park is contained. The major features of the caldera measure about 55 kilometers (34 mi) by 72 kilometers (45 mi) as determined by geological field work conducted by Bob Christiansen of the United States Geological Survey in the 1960s and 1970s.
a. 1703 Genroku earthquake
b. 1700 Cascadia earthquake
c. 1509 Istanbul earthquake
d. Yellowstone caldera

48. A _____ is a cauldron-like volcanic feature usually formed by the collapse of land following a volcanic eruption such as the one at Yellowstone National Park. They are sometimes confused with volcanic craters.
a. 1509 Istanbul earthquake
b. 1700 Cascadia earthquake
c. 1703 Genroku earthquake
d. Caldera

Chapter 6. Streams and Flooding

1. The _____ is an informal name for the supereon comprising the eons of the geologic timescale that came before the current Phanerozoic eon. It spans from the formation of Earth around 4500 Mya (million years ago) to the evolution of abundant macroscopic hard-shelled animals, which marked the beginning of the Cambrian, the first period of the first era of the Phanerozoic eon, some 542 Mya. It is named after the Roman name for Wales - Cambria - where rocks from this age were first studied.
   a. 1509 Istanbul earthquake
   b. Precambrian
   c. 1700 Cascadia earthquake
   d. 1703 Genroku earthquake

2. The _____ describes the continuous movement of water on, above, and below the surface of the Earth. Since the _____ is truly a 'cycle,' there is no beginning or end. Water can change states among liquid, vapor, and ice at various places in the _____.
   a. Surface water
   b. Specific storage
   c. Hydraulic conductivity
   d. Water cycle

3. In geology a _____ is the smallest division of a geologic formation or stratigraphic rock series marked by well-defined divisional planes (bedding planes) separating it from layers above and below. A _____ is the smallest lithostratigraphic unit, usually ranging in thickness from a centimeter to several meters and distinguishable from _____s above and below it. _____s can be differentiated in various ways, including rock or mineral type and particle size.
   a. Biozones
   b. Bed
   c. Cyclostratigraphy
   d. Sequence stratigraphy

4. The term _____ describes particles in a flowing fluid (usually a river) that are transported along the bed. This is in opposition to suspended load and wash load which are carried entirely in suspension.

   _____ moves by a variety of methods, including rolling, sliding, traction, and saltation.

   a. Bed load
   b. Gravitational erosion
   c. Bradyseism
   d. Toreva block

5. _____ is the natural or artificial removal of surface and sub-surface water from an area. Many agricultural soils need _____ to improve production or to manage water supplies.

   The earliest archaeological record of an advanced system of _____ comes from the Indus Valley Civilization from around 3100 BC in what is now Pakistan and North India.

   a. 1703 Genroku earthquake
   b. 1509 Istanbul earthquake
   c. 1700 Cascadia earthquake
   d. Drainage

6. A _____ is an extent of land where water from rain or snow melt drains downhill into a body of water, such as a river, lake, reservoir, estuary, wetland, sea or ocean. The _____ includes both the streams and rivers that convey the water as well as the land surfaces from which water drains into those channels, and is separated from adjacent basins by a drainage divide.

   The _____ acts like a funnel, collecting all the water within the area covered by the basin and channelling it into a waterway.

a. 1703 Genroku earthquake
c. 1700 Cascadia earthquake
b. 1509 Istanbul earthquake
d. Drainage basin

7. In geology, _____ is a specific type of particle transport by fluids such as wind, or the denser fluid water. It occurs when loose material is removed from a bed and carried by the fluid, before being transported back to the surface. Examples include pebble transport by rivers, sand drift over desert surfaces, soil blowing over fields, or even snow drift over smooth surfaces such as those in the Arctic or Canadian Prairies.

a. Transgression
c. Stoping
b. Wave pounding
d. Saltation

8. _____ is any particulate matter that can be transported by fluid flow, and which eventually is deposited.

They are most often transported by water (fluvial processes) transported by wind (aeolian processes) and glaciers. Beach sands and river channel deposits are examples of fluvial transport and deposition, though _____ also often settles out of slow-moving or standing water in lakes and oceans.

a. Sediment
c. Dry quicksand
b. Fech fech
d. Brickearth

9. The phrase _____ is used to describe the movement of solid particles (sediment) and the processes that govern their motion. _____ is typically due to a combination of the force of gravity acting on the sediment, and/or the movement of the fluid in which the sediment is entrained. This is typically studied in natural systems, where the particles are clastic rocks (sand, gravel, boulders, etc.), mud, or clay; the fluid is air, water, or ice; and the force of gravity is due to the sloping surface on which the particles are resting.

a. 1700 Cascadia earthquake
c. 1703 Genroku earthquake
b. 1509 Istanbul earthquake
d. Sediment transport

10. _____ is the term for the fine particles that are light enough to be carried in a stream without touching the stream bed. These particles are generally of the fine sand, silt and clay size, although they can be larger, especially in cases of high discharge, such as during floods. This is in contrast to bed load which is carried along the bottom of the stream.

a. Suspended load
c. Pahoehoe lava
b. Strike-slip faults
d. Valley glaciers

11. _____ is the geological process by which material is added to a landform or land mass. Fluids such as wind and water, as well as sediment gravity flows, transport previously eroded sediment, which, at the loss of enough kinetic energy in the fluid, is deposited, building up layers of sediment.

_____ occurs when the forces responsible for sediment transportation are no longer sufficient to overcome the forces of particle weight and friction, which resist motion.

a. Wave pounding
c. Hydrothermal circulation
b. Seafloor spreading
d. Deposition

12. _____ is the term for material, especially ions from chemical weathering, that are carried in solution by a stream.

a. Dissolved load
b. Lithostatic pressure
c. Transition zone
d. Rill

13. The _____ is the epoch from 1.8 million to 11550 years BP covering the world's recent period of repeated glaciations. The _____ epoch follows the Pliocene epoch and is followed by the Holocene epoch. The _____ is the third epoch of the Neogene period or 6th epoch of the Cenozoic Era. The end of the _____ corresponds with the retreat of the last continental glacier. It also corresponds with the end of the Paleolithic age used in archaeology.
  a. Tyrrhenian
  b. Sicilian Stage
  c. Pleistocene
  d. Late Pleistocene

14. _____, also known as the Pleistocene glaciation, the current ice age or simply the ice age, refers to the period of the last few million years in which permanent ice sheets were established in Antarctica and perhaps Greenland, and fluctuating ice sheets have occurred elsewhere The major effects of the ice age were erosion and deposition of material over large parts of the continents, modification of river systems, creation of millions of lakes, changes in sea level, development of pluvial lakes far from the ice margins, isostatic adjustment of the crust, and abnormal winds. It affected oceans, flooding, and biological communities.
  a. Glacial period
  b. Wolstonian Stage
  c. Bergschrund
  d. Quaternary glaciation

15. An _____ is a fan-shaped deposit formed where a fast flowing stream flattens, slows, and spreads typically at the exit of a canyon onto a flatter plain. A convergence of neighboring fans into a single apron of deposits against a slope is called a bajada, or compound _____.
  a. AASHTO Soil Classification System
  b. AL 333
  c. Alluvial fan
  d. AL 129-1

16. A _____ is flat or nearly flat land adjacent to a stream or river that experiences occasional or periodic flooding. It includes the floodway, which consists of the stream channel and adjacent areas that carry flood flows, and the flood fringe, which are areas covered by the flood, but which do not experience a strong current.

They generally contain unconsolidated sediments, often extending below the bed of the stream.

  a. 1509 Istanbul earthquake
  b. 1700 Cascadia earthquake
  c. 1703 Genroku earthquake
  d. Floodplain

17. A _____ in general is a bend in a sinuous watercourse. A _____ is formed when the moving water in a river erodes the outer banks and widens its valley. A stream of any volume may assume a meandering course, alternatively eroding sediments from the outside of a bend and depositing them on the inside.
  a. 1700 Cascadia earthquake
  b. 1509 Istanbul earthquake
  c. 1703 Genroku earthquake
  d. Meander

18. In physics, chemistry and materials science, _____ concerns the movement and filtering of fluids through porous materials. Examples include the movement of solvents through filter paper (chromatography) and the movement of petroleum through fractured rock. Electrical analogs include the flow of electricity through random resistor networks.
  a. 1700 Cascadia earthquake
  b. 1703 Genroku earthquake
  c. 1509 Istanbul earthquake
  d. Percolation

Chapter 6. Streams and Flooding

19. A _____ is an opening in a planet's surface or crust, which allows hot, molten rock, ash, and gases to escape from below the surface. Volcanic activity involving the extrusion of rock tends to form mountains or features like mountains over a period of time.
    a. 1509 Istanbul earthquake
    b. 1703 Genroku earthquake
    c. Volcano
    d. 1700 Cascadia earthquake

20. _____ is rock that is of a specific particle size range. Specifically, it is any loose rock that is larger than two millimeters (2mm) in its largest dimension (about 1/12 of an inch) and no more than 64 millimeters (about 2.5 inches.) The next smaller size class in geology is sand, which is >0.0625 mm to 2 mm in size.
    a. 1703 Genroku earthquake
    b. 1700 Cascadia earthquake
    c. 1509 Istanbul earthquake
    d. Gravel

21. _____ is the water flow which occurs when soil is infiltrated to full capacity and excess water, from rain, snowmelt, or other sources flows over the land. This is a major component of the hydrologic cycle. Runoff that occurs on surfaces before reaching a channel is also called a nonpoint source.
    a. Thermal pollution
    b. 1509 Istanbul earthquake
    c. 1700 Cascadia earthquake
    d. Surface runoff

22. A _____ is a rapid flooding of geomorphic low-lying areas - washes, rivers and streams. It is caused by heavy rain associated with a thunderstorm, hurricane, or tropical storm. _____ s can also occur after the collapse of an ice dam, or a human structure, such as a dam, for example, the Johnstown Flood of 1889.
    a. Flash flood
    b. 1509 Istanbul earthquake
    c. 1700 Cascadia earthquake
    d. Storm surge

23. _____ is the point at which the surface of a river, creek, or other body of water has risen to a sufficient level to cause damage or affects use of man-made structures. When a body of water rises to this level, it is considered a flood event.

    _____ means a manmade feature is underwater.

    a. Flood stage
    b. Stream capacity
    c. Vadose zone
    d. Specific storage

24. In chronostratigraphy, a _____ is a succession of rock strata laid down in an single age on the geologic timescale, which usually represents millions of years of deposition. A given _____ of rock and the corresponding age of time will by convention have the same name, and the same boundaries.
    a. Chronozone
    b. Relative dating
    c. Global Standard Stratigraphic Age
    d. Stage

25. A _____ or mudslide is the most rapid (up to 80 km/h, or 50 mph) and fluid type of downhill mass wasting. It is a rapid movement of a large mass of mud formed from loose earth and water. Similar terms are mudslide (not very liquid), mud stream, debris flow (e.g. in high mountains), jökulhlaup, and lahar
    a. 1509 Istanbul earthquake
    b. Mudflow
    c. 1703 Genroku earthquake
    d. 1700 Cascadia earthquake

26. The term _____ can be used to describe both the conduct of a survey for geological purposes and an institution holding geological information.

A _____ is the systematic investigation of the subsurface of a given piece of ground for the purpose of creating a geological map or model. A _____ employs techniques from the traditional walk-over survey, studying outcrops and landforms, to intrusive methods, such as hand augering and machine driven boreholes, to the use of geophysical techniques and remote sensing methods, such as aerial photography and satellite imagery.

a. Patterned ground
c. Georeactor

b. Gradualism
d. Geological Survey

27. A _____, dike (or dyke), embankment, floodbank or stopbank is a natural or artificial slope or wall to regulate water levels. It is usually earthen and often parallel to the course of a river or the coast.

a. 1700 Cascadia earthquake
c. 1509 Istanbul earthquake

b. 1703 Genroku earthquake
d. Levee

28. The lithosphere is broken up into what are called _____. In the case of Earth, there are eight major and many minor plates The lithospheric plates ride on the asthenosphere. These plates move in relation to one another at one of three types of plate boundaries: convergent, or collisional boundaries; divergent boundaries, also called spreading centers; and transform boundaries.

a. Panthalassa
c. Tectonic plates

b. Forearc
d. Subduction

Chapter 7. Coastal Zones and Processes

1. The general term '_____' or, more precisely, 'glacial age' denotes a geological period of long-term reduction in the temperature of the Earth's surface and atmosphere, resulting in an expansion of continental ice sheets, polar ice sheets and alpine glaciers. Within a long-term _____, individual pulses of extra cold climate are termed 'glaciations'. Glaciologically, _____ implies the presence of extensive ice sheets in the northern and southern hemispheres; by this definition we are still in an _____

   a. AL 333
   b. AL 129-1
   c. AASHTO Soil Classification System
   d. Ice Age

2. The _____ is a mid-ocean ridge, a divergent tectonic plate boundary located along the floor of the Atlantic Ocean, and the longest mountain range in the world. It separates the Eurasian Plate and North American Plate in the North Atlantic, and the African Plate from the South American Plate in the South Atlantic. The MAR extends from a junction with the Gakkel Ridge (Mid-Arctic Ridge) northeast of Greenland southward to the Bouvet Triple Junction in the South Atlantic.

   a. 1703 Genroku earthquake
   b. Mid-Atlantic Ridge
   c. 1509 Istanbul earthquake
   d. 1700 Cascadia earthquake

3. The _____ is the zone of the ocean floor that separates the thin oceanic crust from thick continental crust. _____s constitute about 28% of the oceanic area.

   The transition from continental to oceanic crust commonly occurs within the outer part of the margin, called continental rise.

   a. 1509 Istanbul earthquake
   b. Swash
   c. Cuspate forelands
   d. Continental margin

4. _____ is the removal of solids (sediment, soil, rock and other particles) in the natural environment. It usually occurs due to transport by wind, water, or ice; by down-slope creep of soil and other material under the force of gravity; or by living organisms, such as burrowing animals, in the case of bioerosion.

   _____ is distinguished from weathering, which is the process of chemical or physical breakdown of the minerals in the rocks, although the two processes may occur concurrently.

   a. AASHTO Soil Classification System
   b. AL 129-1
   c. AL 333
   d. Erosion

5. _____ describes the large scale motions of Earth's lithosphere. The theory encompasses the older concepts of continental drift, developed during the first decades of the 20th century by Alfred Wegener, and seafloor spreading, understood during the 1960s.

   The outermost part of the Earth's interior is made up of two layers: the lithosphere and the asthenosphere.

   a. Continental collision
   b. Plate tectonics
   c. Tectonic plates
   d. Nappe

6. The _____ was proposed by the Danish geological pioneer Nicholas Steno (1638-1686.) This principle states that layers of sediment are originally deposited horizontally. The principle is important to the analysis of folded and tilted strata.

a. Key bed
b. Cyclostratigraphy
c. Bedrock
d. Principle of Original Horizontality

7. _____ is mechanical scraping of a rock surface by friction between rocks and moving particles during their transport in wind, glacier, waves, gravity or running water, after friction, the moving particles dislodge loose and weak debris from the side of the rock, these particles can be dissolved in the water source.

The intensity of _____ depends on the hardness, concentration, velocity and mass of moving particles.

A virtually smooth marine platform cut by the ocean waves at a coastline.

a. AL 129-1
b. AASHTO Soil Classification System
c. AL 333
d. Abrasion

8. The _____ is the maximum depth at which a water wave's passage causes significant water motion. For water depths larger than the _____, bottom sediments are no longer stirred by the wave motion above.

In deep water, the water particles are moved in a circular orbital motion when a wave passes.

a. Wave base
b. 1703 Genroku earthquake
c. 1509 Istanbul earthquake
d. 1700 Cascadia earthquake

9. _____ is the largest volcano on earth in terms of area covered and one of five volcanoes that form the Island of Hawaii in the U.S. state of Hawai>Ê»i in the Pacific Ocean. It is an active shield volcano, with a volume estimated at approximately 18,000 cubic miles (75,000 kmÂ³), although its peak is about 120 feet (37 m) lower than that of its neighbor, Mauna Kea. The Hawaiian name '_____' means 'Long Mountain'.

a. Mauna Loa
b. 1509 Istanbul earthquake
c. 1700 Cascadia earthquake
d. 1703 Genroku earthquake

10. _____ is molten rock expelled by a volcano during eruption. When first expelled from a volcanic vent, it is a liquid at temperatures from 700 >°C to 1,200 >°C (1,300 >°F to 2,200 >°F.) Although _____ is quite viscous, with about 100,000 times the viscosity of water, it can flow great distances before cooling and solidifying, because of both its thixotropic and shear thinning properties.

a. Cinder
b. Lapilli
c. Pit crater
d. Lava

11. A _____ is a natural formation (or landform) where a rock arch forms, with a natural passageway through underneath. Most _____es form as a narrow ridge, walled by cliffs, become narrower from erosion, with a softer rock stratum under the cliff-forming stratum gradually eroding out until the rock shelters thus formed meet underneath the ridge, thus forming the arch. They commonly form where cliffs are subject to erosion from the sea, rivers or weathering (sub-aerial processes); the processes 'find' weaknesses in rocks and work on them, making them bigger until they break through.

a. 1703 Genroku earthquake
b. 1700 Cascadia earthquake
c. Natural arch
d. 1509 Istanbul earthquake

Chapter 7. Coastal Zones and Processes

12. A _____ is a geological landform consisting of a steep and often vertical column or columns of rock in the sea near a coast. They are formed when part of a headland is eroded by hydraulic action, which is the force of the sea or water crashing against the rock. The force of the water weakens cracks in the headland, causing them to later collapse, forming free-standing _____s and even a small island.

   a. Cleavage
   b. Streak
   c. Tarn
   d. Stack

13. A _____ is an opening in a planet's surface or crust, which allows hot, molten rock, ash, and gases to escape from below the surface. Volcanic activity involving the extrusion of rock tends to form mountains or features like mountains over a period of time.

   a. 1509 Istanbul earthquake
   b. 1703 Genroku earthquake
   c. 1700 Cascadia earthquake
   d. Volcano

14. The _____ is the mechanically weak ductily-deforming region of the upper mantle of the Earth. It lies below the lithosphere, at depths between 100 and 200 km (~ 62 and 124 miles) below the surface, but perhaps extending as deep as 400 km (~ 249 miles.)

The _____ is a portion of the upper mantle just below the lithosphere that is involved in plate movements and isostatic adjustments. In spite of its heat, pressures keep it plastic, and it has a relatively low density. Seismic waves pass relatively slowly through the _____, compared to the overlying lithospheric mantle, thus it has been called the low-velocity zone. This was the observation that originally alerted seismologists to its presence and gave some information about its physical properties, as the speed of seismic waves decreases with decreasing rigidity.

   a. Asthenosphere
   b. AASHTO Soil Classification System
   c. AL 129-1
   d. AL 333

15. The _____ is the rigid outermost shell of a rocky planet.

In the Earth, the _____ includes the crust and the uppermost mantle, which constitute the hard and rigid outer layer of the planet. The _____ is underlain by the asthenosphere, the weaker, hotter, and deeper part of the upper mantle.

   a. Forearc
   b. Lithosphere
   c. Gorda Ridge
   d. Subduction

16. In geology, a _____ is a continental area covered by relatively flat or gently tilted, mainly sedimentary strata, which overlie a basement of consolidated igneous or metamorphic rocks of an earlier deformation. They as well as, shields and the basement rocks together constitute cratons.

It is also common practice to use the term _____ as a very general term for a sequence of shallow water carbonate _____.

   a. Nodule
   b. Geothermal
   c. Combe
   d. Platform

17. In geology, engineering, and surveying, _____ is the motion of a surface (usually, the Earth's surface) as it shifts downward relative to a datum such as sea-level. The opposite of _____ is uplift, which results in an increase in elevation. There are several types of _____.
   a. Subsidence
   b. 1700 Cascadia earthquake
   c. Pothole
   d. 1509 Istanbul earthquake

18. The _____ is the epoch from 1.8 million to 11550 years BP covering the world's recent period of repeated glaciations. The _____ epoch follows the Pliocene epoch and is followed by the Holocene epoch. The _____ is the third epoch of the Neogene period or 6th epoch of the Cenozoic Era. The end of the _____ corresponds with the retreat of the last continental glacier. It also corresponds with the end of the Paleolithic age used in archaeology.
   a. Late Pleistocene
   b. Sicilian Stage
   c. Tyrrhenian
   d. Pleistocene

19. _____, also known as the Pleistocene glaciation, the current ice age or simply the ice age, refers to the period of the last few million years in which permanent ice sheets were established in Antarctica and perhaps Greenland, and fluctuating ice sheets have occurred elsewhere The major effects of the ice age were erosion and deposition of material over large parts of the continents, modification of river systems, creation of millions of lakes, changes in sea level, development of pluvial lakes far from the ice margins, isostatic adjustment of the crust, and abnormal winds. It affected oceans, flooding, and biological communities.
   a. Wolstonian Stage
   b. Bergschrund
   c. Glacial period
   d. Quaternary glaciation

20. In geology, _____ is transported rock debris overlying the solid bedrock. The term is also sometimes refers to organic debris so-transported. In the largest sense, it refers to the material left behind by retreating continental glaciers.
   a. Fulgurites
   b. Gibraltar Arc
   c. Duricrust
   d. Drift

21. A _____ is a landform, often referred to as a drowned river valley. _____s are almost always estuaries. _____s form where sea levels rise relative to the land either as a result of eustatic sea level change (where the global sea levels rise), or isostatic sea level change (where the land sinks.)
   a. Ria
   b. 1700 Cascadia earthquake
   c. 1509 Istanbul earthquake
   d. 1703 Genroku earthquake

22. Geologically, a _____ is a long, narrow inlet with steep sides, created in a valley carved by glacial activity.

The seeds of a _____ are laid when a glacier cuts a U-shaped valley through abrasion of the surrounding bedrock by the sediment it carries. Many such valleys were formed during the recent ice age.

   a. 1509 Istanbul earthquake
   b. 1700 Cascadia earthquake
   c. 1703 Genroku earthquake
   d. Fjord

23. _____, sometimes known as shore drift, is a geological process by which sediments such as sand or other materials, move along a beach shore. It uses the process of swash to push the material up the beach and backwash down the beach; until it reaches a groyne or another obstacle.

Chapter 7. Coastal Zones and Processes

Where waves approach the coastline at an angle, when they break their swash pushes beach material up the beach at the same angle.

a. 1509 Istanbul earthquake
b. Swash
c. Cuspate forelands
d. Longshore drift

24. The lithosphere is broken up into what are called _____. In the case of Earth, there are eight major and many minor plates The lithospheric plates ride on the asthenosphere. These plates move in relation to one another at one of three types of plate boundaries: convergent, or collisional boundaries; divergent boundaries, also called spreading centers; and transform boundaries.

a. Panthalassa
b. Forearc
c. Subduction
d. Tectonic plates

25. _____ is a naturally occurring granular material composed of finely divided rock and mineral particles.

As the term is used by geologists, _____ particles range in diameter from 0.0625 (or $>^1\!\!/_{16}$ mm, or 62.5 micrometers) to 2 millimeters. An individual particle in this range size is termed a _____ grain.

a. 1703 Genroku earthquake
b. Sand
c. 1509 Istanbul earthquake
d. 1700 Cascadia earthquake

26. _____ is any particulate matter that can be transported by fluid flow, and which eventually is deposited.

They are most often transported by water (fluvial processes) transported by wind (aeolian processes) and glaciers. Beach sands and river channel deposits are examples of fluvial transport and deposition, though _____ also often settles out of slow-moving or standing water in lakes and oceans.

a. Fech fech
b. Sediment
c. Dry quicksand
d. Brickearth

27. _____ are structures constructed on coasts as part of coastal defence or to protect an anchorage from the effects of weather and longshore drift.

Offshore _____, also called bulkheads, reduce the intensity of wave action in inshore waters and thereby reduce coastal erosion. They are constructed some distance away from the coast or built with one end linked to the coast.

a. 1700 Cascadia earthquake
b. 1703 Genroku earthquake
c. 1509 Istanbul earthquake
d. Breakwaters

Chapter 7. Coastal Zones and Processes

28. In geography and geology, a _____ is a significant vertical, or near vertical, rock exposure. _____s are formed as erosion landforms due to the processes of erosion and weathering that produce them. _____s are common on coasts, in mountainous areas, escarpments and along rivers. _____s are usually formed by rock that is resistant to erosion and weathering. Sedimentary rocks are most likely to form sandstone, limestone, chalk, and dolomite. Igneous rocks, such as granite and basalt also often form _____s.
- a. 1700 Cascadia earthquake
- b. 1509 Istanbul earthquake
- c. 1703 Genroku earthquake
- d. Cliff

29. A _____ zone or _____ area is the interface between land and a stream. Plant communities along the river margins are called _____ vegetation, characterized by hydrophilic plants. _____ zones are significant in ecology, environmental management, and civil engineering because of their role in soil conservation, their biodiversity, and the influence they have on aquatic ecosystems.
- a. 1700 Cascadia earthquake
- b. 1509 Istanbul earthquake
- c. Riparian
- d. 1703 Genroku earthquake

30. _____ -- also known as rip rap, rubble, shot rock or rock armour -- is rock or other material used to armor shorelines, streambeds, bridge abutments, pilings and other shoreline structures against scour, water or ice erosion.

It is made from a variety of rock types, commonly granite, limestone or occasionally concrete rubble from building and paving demolition. It is used to protect coastlines and structures from erosion by the sea, rivers, or streams.

- a. Riprap
- b. Geologic preliminary investigation
- c. Sediment control
- d. Silt fence

31. A _____ is a mountain rising from the ocean seafloor that does not reach to the water's surface (sea level), and thus is not an island. These are typically formed from extinct volcanoes, that rise abruptly and are usually found rising from a seafloor of 1,000-4,000 meters depth. They are defined by oceanographers as independent features that rise to at least 1,000 meters above the seafloor.
- a. 1703 Genroku earthquake
- b. 1700 Cascadia earthquake
- c. 1509 Istanbul earthquake
- d. Seamount

32. A _____ or sandbar is a somewhat linear landform within or extending into a body of water, typically composed of sand, silt or small pebbles. A bar is characteristically long and narrow and develops where a stream or ocean current promotes deposition of granular material, resulting in localized shallowing of the water. Bars can appear in the sea, in a lake, or in a river.

The term _____ can be applied to larger geological units that form off a coastline as part of the process of coastal erosion. These include spits and baymouth bars that form across the front of embayments and rias. A tombolo is a bar that forms an isthmus between an island or offshore rock and a mainland shore.

- a. 1509 Istanbul earthquake
- b. 1700 Cascadia earthquake
- c. Shoal
- d. 1703 Genroku earthquake

33. _____ is the wearing away of land or the removal of beach or dune sediments by wave action, tidal currents, wave currents generated by storms, wind, or fast moving motor craft cause _____, which may take the form of long-term losses of sediment and rocks, or merely the temporary redistribution of coastal sediments; erosion in one location may result in accretion nearby. The study of erosion and sediment redistribution is called 'coastal morphodynamics'.

   a. Coastal erosion
   b. Gravitational erosion
   c. Fault scarp
   d. Fault-block

34. _____ is an offshore rise of water associated with a low pressure weather system, typically a tropical cyclone. _____ is caused primarily by high winds pushing on the ocean's surface. The wind causes the water to pile up higher than the ordinary sea level.

   a. 1700 Cascadia earthquake
   b. Lake breakout
   c. Storm surge
   d. 1509 Istanbul earthquake

35. The _____ is a classification used for most Western Hemisphere tropical cyclones that exceed the intensities of tropical depressions and tropical storms. The scale divides hurricanes into five categories distinguished by the intensities of their sustained winds. In order to be classified as a hurricane, a tropical cyclone must have maximum sustained winds of at least 74 mph (33 m/s; 64 kt; 119 km/h.)

   a. 1703 Genroku earthquake
   b. 1700 Cascadia earthquake
   c. 1509 Istanbul earthquake
   d. Saffir-Simpson Hurricane Scale

Chapter 8. Mass Movements

1. A _____ is a geological phenomenon which includes a wide range of ground movement, such as rock falls, deep failure of slopes and shallow debris flows, which can occur in offshore, coastal and onshore environments. Although the action of gravity is the primary driving force for a _____ to occur, there are other contributing factors affecting the original slope stability. Typically, pre-conditional factors build up specific sub-surface conditions that make the area/slope prone to failure, whereas the actual _____ often requires a trigger before being released.
   a. 1700 Cascadia earthquake
   b. 1509 Istanbul earthquake
   c. Mass wasting
   d. Landslide

2. The _____ was proposed by the Danish geological pioneer Nicholas Steno (1638-1686.) This principle states that layers of sediment are originally deposited horizontally. The principle is important to the analysis of folded and tilted strata.
   a. Bedrock
   b. Principle of Original Horizontality
   c. Cyclostratigraphy
   d. Key bed

3. _____ is the geomorphic process by which soil, regolith, and rock move downslope under the force of gravity. Types of _____ include creep, slides, flows, topples, and falls, each with its own characteristic features, and taking place over timescales from seconds to years. _____ occurs on both terrestrial and submarine slopes, and has been observed on Earth, Mars, and Venus.
   a. Soil liquefaction
   b. Mass wasting
   c. 1700 Cascadia earthquake
   d. 1509 Istanbul earthquake

4. The _____ is an engineering property of granular materials. The _____ is the maximum angle of a stable slope determined by friction, cohesion and the shapes of the particles.

   When bulk granular materials are poured onto a horizontal surface, a conical pile will form. The internal angle between the surface of the pile and the horizontal surface is known as the _____ and is related to the density, surface area, and coefficient of friction of the material.

   a. AL 333
   b. AL 129-1
   c. AASHTO Soil Classification System
   d. Angle of repose

5. _____ are waves that travel through the Earth or other elastic body, for example as the result of an earthquake, explosion, or some other process that imparts forces to the body. _____ are also continually excited on Earth by the incessant pounding of ocean waves (referred to as the microseism) and the wind. _____ are studied by seismologists, and measured by a seismograph, which records the output of a seismometer, or geophone.
   a. Harmonic tremor
   b. Rayleigh waves
   c. Paleoliquefaction
   d. Seismic waves

6. Study of geological _____ is related to the study of structural geology, rock microstructure or rock texture and fault mechanics.

   _____ is the response of a rock to deformation usually by compressive stress and forms particular textures. _____ can be homogeneous or non-homogeneous, and may be pure _____ or simple _____.

   a. Graben
   b. Shear
   c. Transform fault
   d. Michoud fault

Chapter 8. Mass Movements

7. _____ in reference to soil is a term used to describe the maximum strength of soil at which point significant plastic deformation or yielding occurs due to an applied shear stress. There is no definitive '_____' of a soil as it depends on a number of factors affecting the soil at any given time and on the frame of reference, in particular the rate at which the shearing occurs.

Two theories are commonly used to estimate the _____ of a soil depending on the rate of shearing as a frame of reference.

   a. Critical state soil mechanics
   b. Consolidation
   c. Groundwater-related subsidence
   d. Shear strength

8. A _____, denoted > (tau), is defined as a stress which is applied parallel or tangential to a face of a material, as opposed to a normal stress which is applied perpendicularly. In other words, considering that weight is a force, hanging something from a wall creates a _____ on the wall, since the weight of the object is acting parallel to the wall, as opposed to hanging something from the ceiling which creates a normal stress on the ceiling, since the weight is acting perpendicular to the ceiling.

The formula to calculate average _____ is:

where

>τ = the _____
F = the force applied
A = the cross sectional area

Beam shear is defined as the internal _____ of a beam caused by the shear force applied to the beam.

   a. Tensile stress
   b. Shear stress
   c. Thixotropy
   d. Viscosity

9. _____ is soil or rock derived granular material of a grain size between sand and clay. _____ may occur as a soil or as suspended sediment in a surface water body. It may also exist as soil deposited at the bottom of a water body.
   a. 1509 Istanbul earthquake
   b. Silt
   c. 1703 Genroku earthquake
   d. 1700 Cascadia earthquake

10. The field of _____ encompasses the analysis of static and dynamic stability of slopes of earth and rock-fill dams, slopes of other types of embankments, excavated slopes, and natural slopes in soil and soft rock.

Earthen slopes can develop a cut-spherical weakness zone. The probability of this happening can be calculated in advance using a simple 2-D circular analysis package. A primary difficulty with analysis is locating the most-probable slip plane for any given situation. Many landslides have only been analyzed after the fact.

a. Slope stability
b. Soil mechanics
c. Shear strength
d. Critical state soil mechanics

11. A _____ is an opening in a planet's surface or crust, which allows hot, molten rock, ash, and gases to escape from below the surface. Volcanic activity involving the extrusion of rock tends to form mountains or features like mountains over a period of time.
   a. 1700 Cascadia earthquake
   b. 1703 Genroku earthquake
   c. 1509 Istanbul earthquake
   d. Volcano

12. The _____ is the world's third deep geological repository licensed to permanently dispose of transuranic radioactive waste for 10000 years that is left from the research and production of nuclear weapons and nuclear power plants. It is located approximately 26 miles east of Carlsbad, New Mexico, in eastern Eddy County.
   a. 1700 Cascadia earthquake
   b. 1703 Genroku earthquake
   c. 1509 Istanbul earthquake
   d. Waste Isolation Pilot Plant

13. _____ is a naturally occurring material composed primarily of fine-grained minerals, which show plasticity through a variable range of water content, and which can be hardened when dried and/or fired. _____ deposits are mostly composed of _____ minerals (phyllosilicate minerals), minerals which impart plasticity and harden when fired and/or dried, and variable amounts of water trapped in the mineral structure by polar attraction. Organic materials which do not impart plasticity may also be a part of _____ deposits.
   a. 1509 Istanbul earthquake
   b. 1700 Cascadia earthquake
   c. 1703 Genroku earthquake
   d. Clay

14. _____ is the process by which the freezing of water-saturated soil causes the deformation and upward thrust of the ground surface. This process can damage plant roots through breaking or desiccation, cause cracks in pavement, and damage the foundations of buildings, even below the frost line. Moist, fine-grained soil at certain temperatures is most susceptible to _____.
   a. 1700 Cascadia earthquake
   b. 1703 Genroku earthquake
   c. 1509 Istanbul earthquake
   d. Frost heaving

15. _____ is a very soft phyllosilicate mineral that typically forms in microscopic crystals, forming a clay. _____, a member of the smectite family, is a 2:1 clay, meaning that it has 2 tetrahedral sheets sandwiching a central octahedral sheet.
   a. 1700 Cascadia earthquake
   b. 1509 Istanbul earthquake
   c. 1703 Genroku earthquake
   d. Montmorillonite

16. _____ is a unique form of highly sensitive marine clay, with the tendency to change from a relatively stiff condition to a liquid mass when it is disturbed.

Undisturbed _____ resembles a water-saturated gel. When a mass of _____ undergoes sufficient stress, however, it instantly turns into a flowing ooze, a process known as liquefaction.

   a. Boulder clay
   b. Sediment
   c. Fech fech
   d. Quick clay

Chapter 8. Mass Movements

17. _____ are type of elastic wave, also called seismic waves, that can travel through gases, elastic solids and liquids, including the Earth. _____ can be produced by earthquakes and recorded by seismometers.
    a. P-waves
    b. 1703 Genroku earthquake
    c. 1509 Istanbul earthquake
    d. 1700 Cascadia earthquake

18. An _____ is the result of a sudden release of energy in the Earth's crust that creates seismic waves. They are recorded with a seismometer or the related and mostly obsolete Richter magnitude, with a magnitude 3 or lower _____ being mostly imperceptible and magnitude 7 causing serious damage over large areas.
    a. AASHTO Soil Classification System
    b. AL 129-1
    c. AL 333
    d. Earthquake

19. _____, meaning 'new eruption', is a volcano located on the Alaska Peninsula in Katmai National Park and Preserve, about 290 miles (470 km) southwest of Anchorage. Formed in 1912 during one of the largest volcanic eruptions of the 20th century, _____ released 30 times the volume of magma as the 1980 eruption of Mount St. Helens. Map showing volcanoes of Alaska.

One of the largest eruptions of the 20th century occurred in 1912, from June 6 to June 8, to form _____.

    a. 1703 Genroku earthquake
    b. 1700 Cascadia earthquake
    c. 1509 Istanbul earthquake
    d. Novarupta

20. A _____ zone or _____ area is the interface between land and a stream. Plant communities along the river margins are called _____ vegetation, characterized by hydrophilic plants. _____ zones are significant in ecology, environmental management, and civil engineering because of their role in soil conservation, their biodiversity, and the influence they have on aquatic ecosystems.
    a. 1509 Istanbul earthquake
    b. 1700 Cascadia earthquake
    c. 1703 Genroku earthquake
    d. Riparian

21. _____ refers to quantities of rock falling freely from a cliff face. A _____ is a fragment of rock (a block) detached by sliding, toppling, or falling, that falls along a vertical or sub-vertical cliff, proceeds down slope by bouncing and flying along ballistic trajectories or by rolling on talus or debris slopes,'e; (Varnes, 1978.) Alternatively, a '_____ is the natural downward motion of a detached block or series of blocks with a small volume involving free falling, bouncing, rolling, and sliding'.
    a. Cryoseism
    b. Predator trap
    c. Solifluction
    d. Rockfall

22. _____ is a form of mass wasting event that occurs when loosely consolidated materials or rock layers move a short distance down a slope. The landmass and the surface it _____s upon is called a failure surface. When the movement occurs in soil, there is often a distinctive rotational movement to the mass, that cuts vertically through bedding planes (landslides take place along a bedding plane or fault). This rotational movement moves along a curved slip surface of regolith (the failure surface) which overlies bedrock. This results in internal deformation of the moving mass consisting chiefly of overturned folds called 'sheath folds.'
    a. Soil
    b. Topsoil
    c. 1509 Istanbul earthquake
    d. Slump

Chapter 8. Mass Movements

23. _____ is a term given to an accumulation of broken rock fragments at the base of crags, mountain cliffs, or valley shoulders. Landforms associated with these materials are sometimes called _____ slopes or talus piles. These deposits typically have a concave upwards form, while the maximum inclination of such deposits corresponds to the angle of repose of the mean debris size.
   a. Scree
   b. 1703 Genroku earthquake
   c. 1509 Istanbul earthquake
   d. 1700 Cascadia earthquake

24. An _____ is a rapid flow of snow down a slope, from either natural triggers or human activity. Typically occurring in mountainous terrain, an _____ can mix air and water with the descending snow. Powerful _____s have the capability to entrain ice, rocks, trees, and other material on the slope; however _____s are always initiated in snow, are primarily composed of flowing snow, and are distinct from mudslides, rock slides, rock _____s, and serac collapses from an icefall.
   a. AL 129-1
   b. AASHTO Soil Classification System
   c. AL 333
   d. Avalanche

25. A _____ or sandbar is a somewhat linear landform within or extending into a body of water, typically composed of sand, silt or small pebbles. A bar is characteristically long and narrow and develops where a stream or ocean current promotes deposition of granular material, resulting in localized shallowing of the water. Bars can appear in the sea, in a lake, or in a river.

    The term _____ can be applied to larger geological units that form off a coastline as part of the process of coastal erosion. These include spits and baymouth bars that form across the front of embayments and rias. A tombolo is a bar that forms an isthmus between an island or offshore rock and a mainland shore.

   a. 1700 Cascadia earthquake
   b. 1509 Istanbul earthquake
   c. 1703 Genroku earthquake
   d. Shoal

26. An _____ is a downslope viscous flow of fine grained materials that have been saturated with water, and moves under the pull of gravity. They are an intermediate type of mass wasting that is between downhill creep and mudflow. The types of materials that are susceptible to _____s are clay, fine sand and silt, and fine-grained pyroclastic material.
   a. Earthflow
   b. AL 129-1
   c. AL 333
   d. AASHTO Soil Classification System

27. A _____ is a mountain rising from the ocean seafloor that does not reach to the water's surface (sea level), and thus is not an island. These are typically formed from extinct volcanoes, that rise abruptly and are usually found rising from a seafloor of 1,000-4,000 meters depth. They are defined by oceanographers as independent features that rise to at least 1,000 meters above the seafloor.
   a. 1703 Genroku earthquake
   b. Seamount
   c. 1509 Istanbul earthquake
   d. 1700 Cascadia earthquake

28. A _____ or mudslide is the most rapid (up to 80 km/h, or 50 mph) and fluid type of downhill mass wasting. It is a rapid movement of a large mass of mud formed from loose earth and water. Similar terms are mudslide (not very liquid), mud stream, debris flow (e.g. in high mountains), j>ökulhlaup, and lahar
   a. 1509 Istanbul earthquake
   b. 1703 Genroku earthquake
   c. 1700 Cascadia earthquake
   d. Mudflow

29. A _____ is the topographic expression of faulting attributed to the displacement of the land surface by movement along the fault. It can be caused by differential erosion along an old inactive geologic fault (a sort of old rupture) with hard and weak rock, or by a movement on an active fault. In many cases, bluffs form from the upthrown block and can be very steep.
   a. Toreva block
   b. Fault scarp
   c. Shutter ridge
   d. Bradyseism

30. A _____ is a large, slow-moving mass of ice, formed from compacted layers of snow, that slowly deforms and flows in response to gravity and high pressure.

_____ ice is the largest reservoir of fresh water on Earth, and second only to oceans as the largest reservoir of total water.

   a. Deforestation
   b. Greenhouse gases
   c. Glacier
   d. Keeling Curve

Chapter 9. Geology and Climate: Glaciers, Deserts, and Global Climate Trends

1. _____ is partially-compacted n>év>é, a type of snow that has been left over from past seasons and has been recrystallized into a substance denser than n>év>é. It is ice that is at an intermediate stage between snow and glacial ice. _____ has the appearance of wet sugar, but has a hardness that makes it extremely resistant to shovelling. It generally has a density greater than 550 kg/mÂ³ and is often found underneath the snow that accumulates at the head of a glacier.
   a. Glacial plucking
   b. Firn
   c. Bull Lake glaciation
   d. Terminal moraine

2. A _____ is a large, slow-moving mass of ice, formed from compacted layers of snow, that slowly deforms and flows in response to gravity and high pressure.

   _____ ice is the largest reservoir of fresh water on Earth, and second only to oceans as the largest reservoir of total water.
   a. Greenhouse gases
   b. Glacier
   c. Keeling Curve
   d. Deforestation

3. Geologically, a _____ is a long, narrow inlet with steep sides, created in a valley carved by glacial activity.

   The seeds of a _____ are laid when a glacier cuts a U-shaped valley through abrasion of the surrounding bedrock by the sediment it carries. Many such valleys were formed during the recent ice age.
   a. 1700 Cascadia earthquake
   b. Fjord
   c. 1509 Istanbul earthquake
   d. 1703 Genroku earthquake

4. The _____ is a vast body of ice covering 1.71 million km^2, roughly 80% of the surface of Greenland. It is the second largest ice body in the World, after the Antarctic Ice Sheet. The ice sheet is almost 2,400 kilometers long in a north-south direction, and its greatest width is 1,100 kilometers at a latitude of 77>°N, near its northern margin.
   a. 1509 Istanbul earthquake
   b. Greenland ice sheet
   c. 1703 Genroku earthquake
   d. 1700 Cascadia earthquake

5. The general term '_____' or, more precisely, 'glacial age' denotes a geological period of long-term reduction in the temperature of the Earth's surface and atmosphere, resulting in an expansion of continental ice sheets, polar ice sheets and alpine glaciers. Within a long-term _____, individual pulses of extra cold climate are termed 'glaciations'. Glaciologically, _____ implies the presence of extensive ice sheets in the northern and southern hemispheres; by this definition we are still in an _____.
   a. AASHTO Soil Classification System
   b. AL 333
   c. AL 129-1
   d. Ice Age

6. The _____ is the epoch from 1.8 million to 11550 years BP covering the world's recent period of repeated glaciations. The _____ epoch follows the Pliocene epoch and is followed by the Holocene epoch. The _____ is the third epoch of the Neogene period or 6th epoch of the Cenozoic Era. The end of the _____ corresponds with the retreat of the last continental glacier. It also corresponds with the end of the Paleolithic age used in archaeology.
   a. Late Pleistocene
   b. Tyrrhenian
   c. Sicilian Stage
   d. Pleistocene

Chapter 9. Geology and Climate: Glaciers, Deserts, and Global Climate Trends

7. _____, also known as the Pleistocene glaciation, the current ice age or simply the ice age, refers to the period of the last few million years in which permanent ice sheets were established in Antarctica and perhaps Greenland, and fluctuating ice sheets have occurred elsewhere The major effects of the ice age were erosion and deposition of material over large parts of the continents, modification of river systems, creation of millions of lakes, changes in sea level, development of pluvial lakes far from the ice margins, isostatic adjustment of the crust, and abnormal winds. It affected oceans, flooding, and biological communities.

    a. Bergschrund   b. Glacial period
    c. Quaternary glaciation   d. Wolstonian Stage

8. An _____ is an ice mass that covers less than 50 000 km^2 of land area (usually covering a highland area.) Masses of ice covering more than 50 000 km^2 are termed an ice sheet.

They are not constrained by topographical features (i.e., they will lie over the top of mountains) but their dome is usually centred on the highest point of a massif.

    a. Ice cap   b. AASHTO Soil Classification System
    c. AL 129-1   d. AL 333

9. _____ are the largest glaciers, enormous masses of ice that are not visibly affected by the landscape and that cover the entire surface beneath them, except possibly on the margins where they are thinnest. Antarctica and Greenland are the only places where continental _____ currently exist. These regions contain vast quantities of fresh water.

    a. AL 129-1   b. Ice sheets
    c. AL 333   d. AASHTO Soil Classification System

10. _____ is the geological process by which material is added to a landform or land mass. Fluids such as wind and water, as well as sediment gravity flows, transport previously eroded sediment, which, at the loss of enough kinetic energy in the fluid, is deposited, building up layers of sediment.

_____ occurs when the forces responsible for sediment transportation are no longer sufficient to overcome the forces of particle weight and friction, which resist motion.

    a. Deposition   b. Hydrothermal circulation
    c. Wave pounding   d. Seafloor spreading

11. _____ is the removal of solids (sediment, soil, rock and other particles) in the natural environment. It usually occurs due to transport by wind, water, or ice; by down-slope creep of soil and other material under the force of gravity; or by living organisms, such as burrowing animals, in the case of bioerosion.

_____ is distinguished from weathering, which is the process of chemical or physical breakdown of the minerals in the rocks, although the two processes may occur concurrently.

    a. Erosion   b. AL 129-1
    c. AL 333   d. AASHTO Soil Classification System

12. _____ is any particulate matter that can be transported by fluid flow, and which eventually is deposited.

They are most often transported by water (fluvial processes) transported by wind (aeolian processes) and glaciers. Beach sands and river channel deposits are examples of fluvial transport and deposition, though _____ also often settles out of slow-moving or standing water in lakes and oceans.

a. Brickearth
b. Dry quicksand
c. Fech fech
d. Sediment

13. A _____ is an amphitheatre-like valley formed at the head of a glacier by erosion. A _____ is also known as a coombe or coomb in England, a combe or comb in America, a corrie in Scotland and Ireland, and a cwm in Wales, although these terms apply to a specific feature of which several may be found in a _____. The term 'comb' is often found at the end of placenames such as Newcomb and Maycomb, where it is pronounced /kÉ™m/.

a. 1509 Istanbul earthquake
b. 1700 Cascadia earthquake
c. 1703 Genroku earthquake
d. Cirque

14. In geology, _____ is transported rock debris overlying the solid bedrock. The term is also sometimes refers to organic debris so-transported. In the largest sense, it refers to the material left behind by retreating continental glaciers.

a. Duricrust
b. Gibraltar Arc
c. Fulgurites
d. Drift

15. A _____ is a moraine that forms at the end of the glacier called the snout.

They mark the maximum advance of the glacier. An end moraine is at the present boundary of the glacier. They are one of the most prominent types of moraines in the Arctic. One famous _____ is the Giant's Wall in Norway.

a. Terminal moraine
b. Glaciolacustrine deposits
c. Firn
d. Bramertonian Stage

16. A _____ is any glacially formed accumulation of unconsolidated glacial debris (soil and rock) which can occur in currently glaciated and formerly glaciated regions, such as those areas acted upon by a past ice age. This debris may have been plucked off the valley floor as a glacier advanced or it may have fallen off the valley walls as a result of frost wedging. _____s may be composed of silt like glacial flour to large boulders.

a. 1700 Cascadia earthquake
b. 1509 Istanbul earthquake
c. 1703 Genroku earthquake
d. Moraine

17. A _____ is a glacial outwash plain formed of sediments deposited by meltwater at the terminus of a glacier.

_____ are found in glaciated areas, such as Svalbard, Kerguelen Islands, and Iceland. Glaciers and icecaps contain large amounts of silt and sediment, picked up as they erode the underlying rocks when they move slowly downhill, and at the snout of the glacier, meltwater can carry this sediment away from the glacier and deposit it on a broad plain.

a. Monadnock
b. Sandur
c. 1509 Istanbul earthquake
d. Rogen moraine

Chapter 9. Geology and Climate: Glaciers, Deserts, and Global Climate Trends 63

18. _____ is unsorted glacial sediment. Glacial drift is a general term for the coarsely graded and extremely heterogeneous sediments of glacial origin. Glacial _____ is that part of glacial drift which was deposited directly by the glacier. In cases where _____ has been indurated or lithified by subsequent burial into solid rock, it is known as the sedimentary rock tillite.
   a. 1700 Cascadia earthquake   b. 1509 Istanbul earthquake
   c. Till   d. 1703 Genroku earthquake

19. The _____ is a classification used for most Western Hemisphere tropical cyclones that exceed the intensities of tropical depressions and tropical storms. The scale divides hurricanes into five categories distinguished by the intensities of their sustained winds. In order to be classified as a hurricane, a tropical cyclone must have maximum sustained winds of at least 74 mph (33 m/s; 64 kt; 119 km/h.)
   a. 1700 Cascadia earthquake   b. 1509 Istanbul earthquake
   c. Saffir-Simpson Hurricane Scale   d. 1703 Genroku earthquake

20. _____ is mechanical scraping of a rock surface by friction between rocks and moving particles during their transport in wind, glacier, waves, gravity or running water, after friction, the moving particles dislodge loose and weak debris from the side of the rock, these particles can be dissolved in the water source.

The intensity of _____ depends on the hardness, concentration, velocity and mass of moving particles.

A virtually smooth marine platform cut by the ocean waves at a coastline.

   a. AASHTO Soil Classification System   b. AL 333
   c. Abrasion   d. AL 129-1

21. _____ are rocks that have been abraded, pitted, etched, grooved, or polished by wind-driven sand or ice crystals. These geomorphic features are most typically found in arid environments where there is little vegetation to interfere with aeolian particle transport, where there are frequently strong winds, and where there is a steady but not overwhelming supply of sand.

_____ can be abraded to eye-catching natural sculptures.

   a. 1509 Istanbul earthquake   b. Coprolite
   c. Fault breccia   d. Ventifacts

22. The _____ or the Dirty Thirties was a period of severe dust storms causing major ecological and agricultural damage to American and Canadian prairie lands from 1930 to 1936 (in some areas until 1940.) The phenomenon was caused by severe drought coupled with decades of extensive farming without crop rotation or other techniques to prevent erosion. Deep plowing of the virgin topsoil of the Great Plains had killed the natural grasses that normally kept the soil in place and trapped moisture even during periods of drought and high winds.
   a. 1509 Istanbul earthquake   b. Dust Bowl
   c. 1700 Cascadia earthquake   d. 1703 Genroku earthquake

23. A _____ is a desert surface that is covered with closely packed, interlocking angular or rounded rock fragments of pebble and cobble size.

Several theories have been proposed for their formation. The more common theory is that they form by the gradual removal of the sand, dust and other fine grained material by the wind and intermittent rain leaving only the larger fragments behind.

a. 1700 Cascadia earthquake
b. 1703 Genroku earthquake
c. Desert pavement
d. 1509 Istanbul earthquake

24. An _____ is the result of a sudden release of energy in the Earth's crust that creates seismic waves. They are recorded with a seismometer or the related and mostly obsolete Richter magnitude, with a magnitude 3 or lower _____ being mostly imperceptible and magnitude 7 causing serious damage over large areas.
a. AL 333
b. AL 129-1
c. AASHTO Soil Classification System
d. Earthquake

25. _____ pertain to the activity of the winds and more specifically, to the winds' ability to shape the surface of the Earth and other planets. Winds may erode, transport, and deposit materials, and are effective agents in regions with sparse vegetation and a large supply of unconsolidated sediments. Although water is much more powerful than wind, _____ are important in arid environments such as deserts.
a. AL 129-1
b. AASHTO Soil Classification System
c. AL 333
d. Aeolian processes

26. _____ is a homogeneous, typically nonstratified, porous, friable, slightly coherent, often calcareous, fine-grained, silty, pale yellow or buff, windblown (aeolian) sediment. It generally occurs as a widespread blanket deposit that covers areas of hundreds of square kilometers and tens of meters thick. _____ often stands in either steep or vertical faces.
a. 1509 Istanbul earthquake
b. Loess
c. 1700 Cascadia earthquake
d. 1703 Genroku earthquake

27. _____ is a naturally occurring granular material composed of finely divided rock and mineral particles.

As the term is used by geologists, _____ particles range in diameter from 0.0625 (or $>^1\!\!/_{16}$ mm, or 62.5 micrometers) to 2 millimeters. An individual particle in this range size is termed a _____ grain.

a. 1700 Cascadia earthquake
b. 1703 Genroku earthquake
c. 1509 Istanbul earthquake
d. Sand

28. _____ is soil or rock derived granular material of a grain size between sand and clay. _____ may occur as a soil or as suspended sediment in a surface water body. It may also exist as soil deposited at the bottom of a water body.
a. 1700 Cascadia earthquake
b. Silt
c. 1703 Genroku earthquake
d. 1509 Istanbul earthquake

29. A _____ is an opening in a planet's surface or crust, which allows hot, molten rock, ash, and gases to escape from below the surface. Volcanic activity involving the extrusion of rock tends to form mountains or features like mountains over a period of time.

Chapter 9. Geology and Climate: Glaciers, Deserts, and Global Climate Trends

a. 1703 Genroku earthquake
b. 1700 Cascadia earthquake
c. Volcano
d. 1509 Istanbul earthquake

30. A _____ zone or _____ area is the interface between land and a stream. Plant communities along the river margins are called _____ vegetation, characterized by hydrophilic plants. _____ zones are significant in ecology, environmental management, and civil engineering because of their role in soil conservation, their biodiversity, and the influence they have on aquatic ecosystems.
a. 1700 Cascadia earthquake
b. 1509 Istanbul earthquake
c. Riparian
d. 1703 Genroku earthquake

31. _____ is the natural or artificial removal of surface and sub-surface water from an area. Many agricultural soils need _____ to improve production or to manage water supplies.

The earliest archaeological record of an advanced system of _____ comes from the Indus Valley Civilization from around 3100 BC in what is now Pakistan and North India.

a. 1509 Istanbul earthquake
b. 1700 Cascadia earthquake
c. 1703 Genroku earthquake
d. Drainage

32. A _____ is an extent of land where water from rain or snow melt drains downhill into a body of water, such as a river, lake, reservoir, estuary, wetland, sea or ocean. The _____ includes both the streams and rivers that convey the water as well as the land surfaces from which water drains into those channels, and is separated from adjacent basins by a drainage divide.

The _____ acts like a funnel, collecting all the water within the area covered by the basin and channelling it into a waterway.

a. Drainage basin
b. 1700 Cascadia earthquake
c. 1509 Istanbul earthquake
d. 1703 Genroku earthquake

33. _____ consists of clay-sized particles of rock, generated by glacial erosion or by artificial grinding to a similar size. Because the material is very small, it becomes suspended in river water making the water appear cloudy.

If the river flows into a glacial lake, the lake may appear turquoise in color as a result.

a. Wolstonian Stage
b. Cordilleran Ice Sheet
c. Rock flour
d. Bergschrund

34. The _____ is an informal name for the supereon comprising the eons of the geologic timescale that came before the current Phanerozoic eon. It spans from the formation of Earth around 4500 Mya (million years ago) to the evolution of abundant macroscopic hard-shelled animals, which marked the beginning of the Cambrian, the first period of the first era of the Phanerozoic eon, some 542 Mya. It is named after the Roman name for Wales - Cambria - where rocks from this age were first studied.
a. 1509 Istanbul earthquake
b. 1703 Genroku earthquake
c. Precambrian
d. 1700 Cascadia earthquake

35. A _____ is the shadow a rain drop has before it lands on the ground, with respect to prevailing wind direction. In a more geographical sense, a _____ is an area of land that has suffered desertification from proximity to mountain ranges. The mountains block the passage of rain-producing weather systems, casting a 'shadow' of dryness behind them.
 a. 1703 Genroku earthquake
 b. 1700 Cascadia earthquake
 c. 1509 Istanbul earthquake
 d. Rain shadow

36. _____ is the movement of the Earth's continents relative to each other. The hypothesis that continents 'drift' was first put forward by Abraham Ortelius in 1596 and was fully developed by Alfred Wegener in 1912. However, it was not until the development of the theory of plate tectonics in the 1960s, that a sufficient geological explanation of that movement was found.
 a. Continental drift
 b. Subduction
 c. Thrust fault
 d. Plate tectonics

37. _____ was the supercontinent that is theorized to have existed during the Paleozoic and Mesozoic eras about 250 million years ago, before the component continents were separated into their current configuration.

The name was first used by the German originator of the continental drift theory, Alfred Wegener, in the 1920 edition of his book The Origin of Continents and Oceans , in which a postulated supercontinent _____ played a key role.

The single enormous ocean which surrounded Pangaea is known as Panthalassa.

 a. 1703 Genroku earthquake
 b. 1509 Istanbul earthquake
 c. 1700 Cascadia earthquake
 d. Pangea

38. The terms _____ and icehouse Earth refer to the prevailing global climate on a timescale of millions of years.

During a _____ Earth period, the planet's atmosphere contains sufficient _____ gases such as carbon dioxide and methane for ice to be entirely absent from the planet's surface.

During icehouse periods, glaciers are present in fluctuating amounts; variations in the Earth's orbit may result in many ice ages, glacials, and interglacials.

 a. 1703 Genroku earthquake
 b. 1509 Istanbul earthquake
 c. Greenhouse
 d. 1700 Cascadia earthquake

39. In physics, _____ describes any process in which energy emitted by one body travels through a medium or through space, ultimately to be absorbed by another body. Non-physicists often associate the word with ionizing _____, but it can also refer to electromagnetic _____ (i.e., radio waves, infrared light, visible light, ultraviolet light, and X-rays) which can also be ionizing _____, to acoustic _____, or to other more obscure processes. What makes it _____ is that the energy radiates (i.e., it travels outward in straight lines in all directions) from the source.
 a. 1700 Cascadia earthquake
 b. 1703 Genroku earthquake
 c. 1509 Istanbul earthquake
 d. Radiation

40. _____ are gases in an atmosphere that absorb and emit radiation within the thermal infrared range. This process is the fundamental cause of the greenhouse effect. Common _____ in the Earth's atmosphere include water vapor, carbon dioxide, methane, nitrous oxide, ozone, and chlorofluorocarbons.

a. Pacific Decadal Oscillation
b. Little Ice Age
c. Deforestation
d. Greenhouse gases

41. The _____ Era is one of three geologic eras of the Phanerozoic eon. The division of time into eras dates back to Giovanni Arduino, in the 18th century, although his original name for the era now called the '_____' was 'Secondary' (making the modern era the 'Tertiary'.)

The _____ was a time of tectonic, climatic and evolutionary activity. The continents gradually shifted from a state of connectedness into their present configuration; the drifting provided for speciation and other important evolutionary developments.

a. 1703 Genroku earthquake
b. 1700 Cascadia earthquake
c. 1509 Istanbul earthquake
d. Mesozoic

42. _____ is a large 13 kilometres wide caldera situated to the west of Naples, Italy declared regional park in 2003. Today mostly lying underwater, the area comprises 24 craters and volcanic edifices, some of which present hydrothermal activity at Lucrino, Agnano and the town of Pozzuoli and effusive gaseous manifestations like the Solfatara crater, mythological home of the Roman god of fire, Vulcan. The area also features bradyseismic phenomena, which are most evident at the temple of Serapis in Pozzuoli.

a. 1700 Cascadia earthquake
b. 1703 Genroku earthquake
c. 1509 Istanbul earthquake
d. Campi Flegrei

43. _____ is a process that converts carbon dioxide into organic compounds, especially sugars, using the energy from sunlight. _____ occurs in plants, algae, and many species of bacteria. With the exception of some bacteria, all use water and carbon dioxide as initial substrates and release oxygen as a waste product.

a. 1509 Istanbul earthquake
b. 1700 Cascadia earthquake
c. Photosynthesis
d. 1703 Genroku earthquake

44. An _____ is an oceanographic phenomenon that involves wind-driven motion of dense, cooler, and usually nutrient-rich water towards the ocean surface, replacing the warmer, usually nutrient-depleted surface water. There are at least five types of _____: coastal _____, large-scale wind-driven _____ in the ocean interior, _____ associated with eddies, topographically-associated _____, and broad-diffusive _____ in the ocean interior.

Coastal _____ is the best known type of _____, and the most closely related to human activities as it supports some of the most productive fisheries in the world, like small pelagics (sardines, anchovies, etc.).

a. AL 333
b. AL 129-1
c. AASHTO Soil Classification System
d. Upwelling

45. The _____ is a pattern of Pacific climate variability that shifts phases on at least inter-decadal time scale, usually about 20 to 30 years. The _____ is detected as warm or cool surface waters in the Pacific Ocean, north of 20>° N. During a 'warm', or 'positive', phase, the west Pacific becomes cool and part of the eastern ocean warms; during a 'cool' or 'negative' phase, the opposite pattern occurs.

a. Greenhouse gases
b. Deforestation
c. Pacific Decadal Oscillation
d. Keeling Curve

Chapter 9. Geology and Climate: Glaciers, Deserts, and Global Climate Trends

46. _____ is the consumption of energy or power. It is covered in the following articles and categories:

- World energy resources and consumption
- Domestic _____
- Efficient energy use
- Energy conservation, the practice of decreasing the quantity of energy used

a. AL 333
b. AL 129-1
c. AASHTO Soil Classification System
d. Energy consumption

47. _____ is a pattern of resource use that aims to meet human needs while preserving the environment so that these needs can be met not only in the present, but also for future generations. The term was used by the Brundtland Commission which coined what has become the most often-quoted definition of _____ as development that 'meets the needs of the present without compromising the ability of future generations to meet their own needs.'

_____ ties together concern for the carrying capacity of natural systems with the social challenges facing humanity. As early as the 1970s 'sustainability' was employed to describe an economy 'in equilibrium with basic ecological support systems.' Ecologists have pointed to the 'limits of growth' and presented the alternative of a 'steady state economy' in order to address environmental concerns.

a. 1703 Genroku earthquake
b. 1700 Cascadia earthquake
c. 1509 Istanbul earthquake
d. Sustainable development

Chapter 10. Water as a Resource

1. The _____ provides a uniform system of measuring pollution levels for the major air pollutants. It is based on a scale devised by the United States Environmental Protection Agency (USEPA) to provide a way for broadcasts and newspapers to report air quality on a daily basis.

The _____ is reported as a number on a scale of 0 to 500 and is the air quality indicator.

   a. 1703 Genroku earthquake
   b. 1700 Cascadia earthquake
   c. Pollutant Standards Index
   d. 1509 Istanbul earthquake

2. A _____ zone or _____ area is the interface between land and a stream. Plant communities along the river margins are called _____ vegetation, characterized by hydrophilic plants. _____ zones are significant in ecology, environmental management, and civil engineering because of their role in soil conservation, their biodiversity, and the influence they have on aquatic ecosystems.
   a. 1700 Cascadia earthquake
   b. 1509 Istanbul earthquake
   c. 1703 Genroku earthquake
   d. Riparian

3. The _____ is the world's third deep geological repository licensed to permanently dispose of transuranic radioactive waste for 10000 years that is left from the research and production of nuclear weapons and nuclear power plants. It is located approximately 26 miles east of Carlsbad, New Mexico, in eastern Eddy County.
   a. 1703 Genroku earthquake
   b. Waste Isolation Pilot Plant
   c. 1509 Istanbul earthquake
   d. 1700 Cascadia earthquake

4. An _____ is the result of a sudden release of energy in the Earth's crust that creates seismic waves. They are recorded with a seismometer or the related and mostly obsolete Richter magnitude, with a magnitude 3 or lower _____ being mostly imperceptible and magnitude 7 causing serious damage over large areas.
   a. AL 129-1
   b. AL 333
   c. AASHTO Soil Classification System
   d. Earthquake

5. _____ is the result of the transformation of an existing rock type, the protolith, in a process called metamorphism, which means 'change in form'. The protolith is subjected to heat and pressure (temperatures greater than 150 to 200 >°C and pressures of 1500 bars) causing profound physical and/or chemical change. The protolith may be sedimentary rock, igneous rock or another older _____.
   a. Metavolcanic rock
   b. Metamorphic rock
   c. Serpentinite
   d. Rock cycle

6. _____ in the earth sciences (commonly symbolized as κ a rock or k) is a measure of the ability of a material (typically unconsolidated material) to transmit fluids. It is of great importance in determining the flow characteristics of hydrocarbons in oil and gas reservoirs, and of groundwater in aquifers. It is typically measured in the lab by application of Darcy's law under steady state conditions or, more generally, by application of various solutions to the diffusion equation for unsteady flow conditions.
   a. Permeability
   b. Porosity
   c. Saltwater intrusion
   d. Phreatic zone

7. _____ is a measure of the void spaces in a material, and is measured as a fraction, between 0-1, or as a percentage between 0-100%. The term is used in multiple fields including ceramics, metallurgy, materials, manufacturing, earth sciences and construction.

Used in geology, hydrogeology, soil science, and building science, the _____ of a porous medium (such as rock or sediment) describes the fraction of void space in the material, where the void may contain, for example, air or water.

a. Permeability
c. Saltwater intrusion
b. Phreatic zone
d. Porosity

8. _____ is the naturally occurring, unconsolidated or loose covering on the Earth's surface. _____ is composed of particles of broken rock that have been altered by chemical, biological and environmental processes including weathering and erosion. _____ is different from its parent rock(s) source(s), altered by interactions between the lithosphere, hydrosphere, atmosphere, and the biosphere.

a. Slump
c. Topsoil
b. 1509 Istanbul earthquake
d. Soil

9. The _____ or the Dirty Thirties was a period of severe dust storms causing major ecological and agricultural damage to American and Canadian prairie lands from 1930 to 1936 (in some areas until 1940.) The phenomenon was caused by severe drought coupled with decades of extensive farming without crop rotation or other techniques to prevent erosion. Deep plowing of the virgin topsoil of the Great Plains had killed the natural grasses that normally kept the soil in place and trapped moisture even during periods of drought and high winds.

a. 1700 Cascadia earthquake
c. Dust Bowl
b. 1509 Istanbul earthquake
d. 1703 Genroku earthquake

10. _____ is a large 13 kilometres wide caldera situated to the west of Naples, Italy declared regional park in 2003. Today mostly lying underwater, the area comprises 24 craters and volcanic edifices, some of which present hydrothermal activity at Lucrino, Agnano and the town of Pozzuoli and effusive gaseous manifestations like the Solfatara crater, mythological home of the Roman god of fire, Vulcan. The area also features bradyseismic phenomena, which are most evident at the temple of Serapis in Pozzuoli.

a. 1700 Cascadia earthquake
c. Campi Flegrei
b. 1703 Genroku earthquake
d. 1509 Istanbul earthquake

11. _____ is water located beneath the ground surface in soil pore spaces and in the fractures of lithologic formations. A unit of rock or an unconsolidated deposit is called an aquifer when it can yield a usable quantity of water. The depth at which soil pore spaces or fractures and voids in rock become completely saturated with water is called the water table.

a. 1700 Cascadia earthquake
c. Depression focused recharge
b. 1509 Istanbul earthquake
d. Groundwater

12. The _____ is the area in an aquifer, below the water table, in which relatively all pores and fractures are saturated with water. The _____ may fluctuate with changes of season and during wet and dry periods.

a. Permeability
c. Saltwater intrusion
b. Phreatic zone
d. Porosity

Chapter 10. Water as a Resource

13. _____ or moisture content is the quantity of water contained in a material, such as soil (called soil moisture), rock, ceramics, or wood on a volumetric or gravimetric basis. The property is used in a wide range of scientific and technical areas, and is expressed as a ratio, which can range from 0 (completely dry) to the value of the materials' porosity at saturation.

Volumetric _____, θ, is defined mathematically as:

$$\theta = \frac{V_w}{V_T}$$

where V_w is the volume of water and $V_T = V_s + V_v = V_s + V_w + V_a$ is the total volume (that is Soil Volume + Water Volume + Void Space.)

   a. Trace element
   b. 1700 Cascadia earthquake
   c. 1509 Istanbul earthquake
   d. Water content

14. The _____, also termed the unsaturated zone, is the portion of Earth between the land surface and the phreatic zone or zone of saturation . It extends from the top of the ground surface to the water table. Water in the _____ has a pressure head less than atmospheric pressure, and is retained by a combination of adhesion , and capillary action (capillary groundwater.)
   a. Surface water
   b. Stemflow
   c. Vadose zone
   d. Specific storage

15. The _____ is the level at which the ground water pressure is equal to atmospheric pressure. It may be conveniently visualized as the 'surface' of the ground water in a given vicinity. It usually coincides with the phreatic surface, but can be many feet above it. As water infiltrates through pore spaces in the soil, it first passes through the zone of aeration, where the soil is unsaturated. At increasing depths water fills in more spaces, until the zone of saturation is reached. The relatively horizontal plane atop this zone constitutes the _____.
   a. Rock bolt
   b. Shaft construction
   c. Crosshole sonic logging
   d. Water table

16. An _____ is an underground layer of water-bearing permeable rock or unconsolidated materials (gravel, sand, silt, or clay) from which groundwater can be usefully extracted using a water well. The study of water flow in _____s and the characterization of _____s is called hydrogeology. Related terms include: an aquitard, which is an impermeable layer along an _____, and an aquiclude (or aquifuge), which is a solid, impermeable area beneath an _____.
   a. AL 333
   b. AL 120 1
   c. AASHTO Soil Classification System
   d. Aquifer

17. _____ is the movement of the Earth's continents relative to each other. The hypothesis that continents 'drift' was first put forward by Abraham Ortelius in 1596 and was fully developed by Alfred Wegener in 1912. However, it was not until the development of the theory of plate tectonics in the 1960s, that a sufficient geological explanation of that movement was found.
   a. Plate tectonics
   b. Subduction
   c. Continental drift
   d. Thrust fault

18. In geology, _____ is transported rock debris overlying the solid bedrock. The term is also sometimes refers to organic debris so-transported. In the largest sense, it refers to the material left behind by retreating continental glaciers.
   a. Fulgurites
   b. Duricrust
   c. Gibraltar Arc
   d. Drift

19. An _____ is a confined aquifer containing groundwater that will flow upward through a well without the need for pumping. Water may even reach the ground surface if the natural pressure is high enough, in which case the well is called a flowing artesian well. An aquifer provides the water for an artesian well.
   a. AL 333
   b. AL 129-1
   c. Artesian aquifer
   d. AASHTO Soil Classification System

20. A _____ is based on hydraulic principles. For an example, we know that two connected storage tanks with one full and one empty will gradually fill/drain to the same level. This is because of atmospheric pressure and gravity.
   a. 1703 Genroku earthquake
   b. 1700 Cascadia earthquake
   c. Potentiometric surface
   d. 1509 Istanbul earthquake

21. A _____ occurs in an aquifer when groundwater is pumped from a well. In an unconfined (water table) aquifer, this is an actual depression of the water levels. In confined (artesian) aquifers, the _____ is a reduction in the pressure head surrounding the pumped well.
   a. Stemflow
   b. Vadose zone
   c. Cone of depression
   d. Stream capacity

22. _____ in geology is a landform sunken or depressed below the surrounding area. _____s may be formed by various mechanisms, and may be referred to by a variety of technical terms.

   - A basin may be any large sediment filled _____. In tectonics, it may refer specifically to a circular, syncline-like _____: a geologic basin; while in sedimentology, it may refer to an area thickly filled with sediment: sedimentary basin.

   - A blowout is a _____ created by wind erosion typically in either a desert sand or dry soil (such as a post-glacial loess environment.)

   - A graben is a down dropped and typically linear _____ or basin created by rifting in a region under tensional tectonic forces.

   - An impact crater is a _____ created by an impact such as a meteorite crater.
   - A pit crater is a _____ formed by a sinking, or caving in, of the ground surface lying over a void.
   - A kettle is left behind when a piece of ice left behind in glacial deposits melts.

   - A _____ may be an area of subsidence caused by the collapse of an underlying structure. Examples include sinkholes above caves in karst topography, or calderas.

   a. Deformation
   b. Fault
   c. Dali
   d. Depression

Chapter 10. Water as a Resource

23. The _____ characterizes the scratch resistance of various minerals through the ability of a harder material to scratch a softer material. It was created in 1812 by the German mineralogist Friedrich Mohs and is one of several definitions of hardness in materials science. The method, however, is of great antiquity, having first been mentioned by Theophrastus in his treatise On Stones in ca 300 BC, followed by Pliny the Elder in his Naturalis Historia circa A.D.
     a. 1700 Cascadia earthquake
     b. 1509 Istanbul earthquake
     c. Mohs scale of mineral hardness
     d. 1703 Genroku earthquake

24. _____ refers to the process by which a sediment progressively loses its porosity due to the effects of loading. This forms part of the process of lithification. When a layer of sediment is originally deposited, it contains an open framework of particles with the pore space being usually filled with water.
     a. Cohesion
     b. Cleavage
     c. Platform
     d. Compaction

25. In geology, engineering, and surveying, _____ is the motion of a surface (usually, the Earth's surface) as it shifts downward relative to a datum such as sea-level. The opposite of _____ is uplift, which results in an increase in elevation. There are several types of _____.
     a. 1509 Istanbul earthquake
     b. Pothole
     c. 1700 Cascadia earthquake
     d. Subsidence

26. In geology, an _____ is a body of igneous rock that has crystallized from molten magma below the surface of the Earth. Bodies of magma that solidify underground before they reach the surface of the earth are called plutons the Roman god of the underworld. Correspondingly, rocks of this kind are also referred to as igneous plutonic rocks or igneous intrusive rocks.
     a. AL 333
     b. AL 129-1
     c. AASHTO Soil Classification System
     d. Intrusion

27. _____ is the movement of saline water into freshwater aquifers. Most often, it is caused by ground-water pumping from coastal wells, or from construction of navigation channels or oil field canals. The channels and canals provide conduits for salt water to be brought into fresh water marshes.
     a. Phreatic zone
     b. Permeability
     c. Porosity
     d. Saltwater intrusion

28. _____ is soil or rock derived granular material of a grain size between sand and clay. _____ may occur as a soil or as suspended sediment in a surface water body. It may also exist as soil deposited at the bottom of a water body.
     a. 1703 Genroku earthquake
     b. Silt
     c. 1509 Istanbul earthquake
     d. 1700 Cascadia earthquake

29. A _____ is a natural depression or hole in the surface topography caused by the removal of soil or bedrock, often both, by water. They may vary in size from less than a meter to several hundred meters both in diameter and depth, and vary in form from soil-lined bowls to bedrock-edged chasms. They may be formed gradually or suddenly, and are found worldwide.
     a. 1700 Cascadia earthquake
     b. 1509 Istanbul earthquake
     c. 1703 Genroku earthquake
     d. Sinkhole

Chapter 10. Water as a Resource

30. A _____ is an opening in a planet's surface or crust, which allows hot, molten rock, ash, and gases to escape from below the surface. Volcanic activity involving the extrusion of rock tends to form mountains or features like mountains over a period of time.
    a. Volcano
    b. 1703 Genroku earthquake
    c. 1509 Istanbul earthquake
    d. 1700 Cascadia earthquake

31. A _____ or sandbar is a somewhat linear landform within or extending into a body of water, typically composed of sand, silt or small pebbles. A bar is characteristically long and narrow and develops where a stream or ocean current promotes deposition of granular material, resulting in localized shallowing of the water. Bars can appear in the sea, in a lake, or in a river.

The term _____ can be applied to larger geological units that form off a coastline as part of the process of coastal erosion. These include spits and baymouth bars that form across the front of embayments and rias. A tombolo is a bar that forms an isthmus between an island or offshore rock and a mainland shore.

    a. 1703 Genroku earthquake
    b. 1700 Cascadia earthquake
    c. Shoal
    d. 1509 Istanbul earthquake

32. A _____ is a mountain rising from the ocean seafloor that does not reach to the water's surface (sea level), and thus is not an island. These are typically formed from extinct volcanoes, that rise abruptly and are usually found rising from a seafloor of 1,000-4,000 meters depth. They are defined by oceanographers as independent features that rise to at least 1,000 meters above the seafloor.
    a. 1509 Istanbul earthquake
    b. Seamount
    c. 1703 Genroku earthquake
    d. 1700 Cascadia earthquake

33. _____ is a landscape shaped by the dissolution of a layer or layers of soluble bedrock, usually carbonate rock such as limestone or dolomite.

Due to subterranean drainage, there may be very limited surface water, even to the absence of all rivers and lakes. Many karst regions display distinctive surface features, with sinkholes or dolines being the most common.

    a. Karst topography
    b. Amblypoda
    c. Andrija Mohorovičić
    d. Ambulocetus

34. 'Parts-per' notation is used, especially in science and engineering, to denote relative proportions in measured quantities; particularly in low-value (high-ratio) proportions at the parts-per-million (ppm), parts-per-billion (ppb), and parts-per-trillion (ppt) level. Since _____s are quantity-per-quantity measures, they are known as dimensionless quantities; that is, they are pure numbers with no associated units of measurement. In regular prose, _____s generally take the literal 'parts per' meaning of a comparative ratio.
    a. Trace element
    b. 1700 Cascadia earthquake
    c. Parts-per notation
    d. 1509 Istanbul earthquake

Chapter 10. Water as a Resource

35. _____ is an expression for the combined content of all inorganic and organic substances contained in a liquid which are present in a molecular, ionized or micro-granular (colloidal sol) suspended form. Generally the operational definition is that the solids must be small enough to survive filtration through a sieve size of two micrometres. _____ are normally only discussed for freshwater systems, since salinity comprises some of the ions constituting the definition of _____.
   a. 1703 Genroku earthquake
   b. 1700 Cascadia earthquake
   c. 1509 Istanbul earthquake
   d. Total dissolved solids

36. _____ is the physical, chemical and biological characteristics of water. It is most frequently used by reference to a set of standards against which compliance can be assessed. The most common standards used to assess _____ relate to drinking water, safety of human contact, and for health of ecosystems.
   a. 1700 Cascadia earthquake
   b. Water quality
   c. Hydraulic head
   d. 1509 Istanbul earthquake

37. The _____ is a vast yet shallow underground water table aquifer located beneath the Great Plains in the United States. One of the world's largest aquifers, it covers an area of approximately 174,000 mi^2 in portions of the eight states of South Dakota, Nebraska, Wyoming, Colorado, Kansas, Oklahoma, New Mexico, and Texas. It was named in 1898 by N.H. Darton from its type locality near the town of Ogallala, Nebraska.
   a. AASHTO Soil Classification System
   b. AL 129-1
   c. AL 333
   d. Ogallala Aquifer

38. _____ is water that has high mineral content (mainly calcium and magnesium ions) (in contrast with soft water.) _____ minerals primarily consist of calcium (Ca^{2+}), and magnesium (Mg^{2+}) metal cations, and sometimes other dissolved compounds such as bicarbonates and sulfates. Calcium usually enters the water as either calcium carbonate ($CaCO_3$), in the form of limestone and chalk, or calcium sulfate ($CaSO_4$), in the form of other mineral deposits.
   a. 1700 Cascadia earthquake
   b. Water quality
   c. 1509 Istanbul earthquake
   d. Hard water

39. _____ is an exchange of ions between two electrolytes or between an electrolyte solution and a complex. In most cases the term is used to denote the processes of purification, separation, and decontamination of aqueous and other ion-containing solutions with solid polymeric or mineralic 'ion exchangers'. _____ resin beads.

Typical ion exchangers are _____ resins (functionalized porous or gel polymer), zeolites, montmorillonite, clay, and soil humus.

   a. AASHTO Soil Classification System
   b. AL 333
   c. AL 129-1
   d. Ion exchange

40. _____ is water collecting on the ground or in a stream, river, lake, wetland, or ocean; it is related to water collecting as groundwater or atmospheric water.

_____ is naturally replenished by precipitation and naturally lost through discharge to evaporation, and sub-surface seepage into the groundwater. Although there are other sources of groundwater, such as connate water and magmatic water, precipitation is the major one and groundwater originated in this way is called meteoric water.

a. Vadose zone
b. Flood stage
c. Cone of depression
d. Surface water

41. _____s are microporous, aluminosilicate minerals commonly used as commercial adsorbents. The term _____ was originally coined in 1756 by Swedish mineralogist Axel Fredrik Cronstedt, who observed that upon rapidly heating the material stilbite, it produced large amounts of steam from water that had been adsorbed by the material. Based on this, he called the material _____, from the Greek ζίω , meaning 'boil' and λῖθος (lithos), meaning 'stone'.

a. 1509 Istanbul earthquake
b. 1700 Cascadia earthquake
c. 1703 Genroku earthquake
d. Zeolite

42. _____ was a physicist and chemist of Polish upbringing and, subsequently, French citizenship. She was a pioneer in the field of radioactivity, the first person honored with two Nobel Prizes, and the first female professor at the University of Paris.

She was born Maria Skłodowska in Warsaw and lived there until she was 24.

a. Andrija Mohorovičić
b. Amblypoda
c. Ambulocetus
d. Marie Skłodowska Curie

43. In geology, _____ refers to heat sources within the planet. _____ is technically an adjective (e.g., _____ energy) but in U.S. English the word has attained frequent use as a noun .

The planet's internal heat was originally generated during its accretion, due to gravitational binding energy, and since then additional heat has continued to be generated by decay heat from the radioactive decay of elements.

a. Fault
b. Platform
c. Geothermal
d. Diamond Head

44. In physics, _____ describes any process in which energy emitted by one body travels through a medium or through space, ultimately to be absorbed by another body. Non-physicists often associate the word with ionizing _____, but it can also refer to electromagnetic _____ (i.e., radio waves, infrared light, visible light, ultraviolet light, and X-rays) which can also be ionizing _____, to acoustic _____, or to other more obscure processes. What makes it _____ is that the energy radiates (i.e., it travels outward in straight lines in all directions) from the source.

a. 1703 Genroku earthquake
b. 1509 Istanbul earthquake
c. 1700 Cascadia earthquake
d. Radiation

45. The _____ is an informal name for the supereon comprising the eons of the geologic timescale that came before the current Phanerozoic eon. It spans from the formation of Earth around 4500 Mya (million years ago) to the evolution of abundant macroscopic hard-shelled animals, which marked the beginning of the Cambrian, the first period of the first era of the Phanerozoic eon, some 542 Mya. It is named after the Roman name for Wales - Cambria - where rocks from this age were first studied.

a. 1703 Genroku earthquake
b. 1509 Istanbul earthquake
c. Precambrian
d. 1700 Cascadia earthquake

Chapter 10. Water as a Resource

46. A _____ is an extent of land where water from rain or snow melt drains downhill into a body of water, such as a river, lake, reservoir, estuary, wetland, sea or ocean. The _____ includes both the streams and rivers that convey the water as well as the land surfaces from which water drains into those channels, and is separated from adjacent basins by a drainage divide.

The _____ acts like a funnel, collecting all the water within the area covered by the basin and channelling it into a waterway.

   a. 1509 Istanbul earthquake
   c. 1700 Cascadia earthquake
   b. 1703 Genroku earthquake
   d. Drainage basin

47. _____ is the geological process by which material is added to a landform or land mass. Fluids such as wind and water, as well as sediment gravity flows, transport previously eroded sediment, which, at the loss of enough kinetic energy in the fluid, is deposited, building up layers of sediment.

_____ occurs when the forces responsible for sediment transportation are no longer sufficient to overcome the forces of particle weight and friction, which resist motion.

   a. Deposition
   c. Hydrothermal circulation
   b. Wave pounding
   d. Seafloor spreading

48. The term _____ can be used to describe both the conduct of a survey for geological purposes and an institution holding geological information.

A _____ is the systematic investigation of the subsurface of a given piece of ground for the purpose of creating a geological map or model. A _____ employs techniques from the traditional walk-over survey, studying outcrops and landforms, to intrusive methods, such as hand augering and machine driven boreholes, to the use of geophysical techniques and remote sensing methods, such as aerial photography and satellite imagery.

   a. Geological Survey
   c. Georeactor
   b. Gradualism
   d. Patterned ground

Chapter 11. Soil as a Resource

1. Two important classifications of weathering processes exist -- physical and _____. Mechanical or physical weathering involves the breakdown of rocks and soils through direct contact with atmospheric conditions, such as heat, water, ice and pressure. The second classification, _____, involves the direct effect of atmospheric chemicals or biologically produced chemicals (also known as biological weathering) in the breakdown of rocks, soils and minerals.
    a. Chemical weathering
    b. Weathering
    c. 1509 Istanbul earthquake
    d. Physical weathering

2. _____ is the removal of solids (sediment, soil, rock and other particles) in the natural environment. It usually occurs due to transport by wind, water, or ice; by down-slope creep of soil and other material under the force of gravity; or by living organisms, such as burrowing animals, in the case of bioerosion.

    _____ is distinguished from weathering, which is the process of chemical or physical breakdown of the minerals in the rocks, although the two processes may occur concurrently.

    a. AL 129-1
    b. AL 333
    c. AASHTO Soil Classification System
    d. Erosion

3. _____ is molten rock that is found beneath the surface of the Earth, and may also exist on other terrestrial planets. Besides molten rock, _____ may also contain suspended crystals and gas bubbles. _____ often collects in a _____ chamber inside a volcano. _____ is capable of intrusion into adjacent rocks, extrusion onto the surface as lava, and explosive ejection as tephra to form pyroclastic rock.
    a. Magma
    b. Volcanic rock
    c. Laccolith
    d. Pluton

4. Two important classifications of weathering processes exist -- _____ and chemical weathering. Mechanical or _____ involves the breakdown of rocks and soils through direct contact with atmospheric conditions, such as heat, water, ice and pressure. The second classification, chemical weathering, involves the direct effect of atmospheric chemicals or biologically produced chemicals (also known as biological weathering) in the breakdown of rocks, soils and minerals.
    a. Weathering
    b. 1509 Istanbul earthquake
    c. Frost disintegration
    d. Physical weathering

5. _____ is a layer of loose, heterogeneous material covering solid rock. It includes dust, soil, broken rock, and other related materials and is present on Earth, the Moon, some asteroids, and other planets. The term was first defined by George P. Merrill in 1897 who stated, 'In places this covering is made up of material originating through rock-weathering or plant growth in situ. In other instances it is of fragmental and more or less decomposed matter drifted by wind, water or ice from other sources. This entire mantle of unconsolidated material, whatever its nature or origin, it is proposed to call the _____.'
    a. 1703 Genroku earthquake
    b. 1509 Istanbul earthquake
    c. 1700 Cascadia earthquake
    d. Regolith

6. _____ is one of the three main rock types (the others being igneous and metamorphic rock.) _____ is formed by deposition and consolidation of mineral and organic material and from precipitation of minerals from solution. The processes that form _____ occur at the surface of the Earth and within bodies of water.
    a. Laccolith
    b. Vesicular texture
    c. Pluton
    d. Sedimentary rock

Chapter 11. Soil as a Resource

7. _____ is the naturally occurring, unconsolidated or loose covering on the Earth's surface. _____ is composed of particles of broken rock that have been altered by chemical, biological and environmental processes including weathering and erosion. _____ is different from its parent rock(s) source(s), altered by interactions between the lithosphere, hydrosphere, atmosphere, and the biosphere.
   a. Soil
   b. Topsoil
   c. 1509 Istanbul earthquake
   d. Slump

8. _____ is the decomposition of Earth rocks, soils and their minerals through direct contact with the planet's atmosphere. _____ occurs in situ, or 'with no movement', and thus should not be confused with erosion, which involves the movement of rocks and minerals by agents such as water, ice, wind and gravity.

Two important classifications of _____ processes exist -- physical and chemical _____.

   a. 1509 Istanbul earthquake
   b. Physical weathering
   c. Frost disintegration
   d. Weathering

9. _____ are type of elastic wave, also called seismic waves, that can travel through gases, elastic solids and liquids, including the Earth. _____ can be produced by earthquakes and recorded by seismometers.
   a. 1509 Istanbul earthquake
   b. P-waves
   c. 1703 Genroku earthquake
   d. 1700 Cascadia earthquake

10. The _____ was proposed by the Danish geological pioneer Nicholas Steno (1638-1686.) This principle states that layers of sediment are originally deposited horizontally. The principle is important to the analysis of folded and tilted strata.
    a. Cyclostratigraphy
    b. Principle of Original Horizontality
    c. Bedrock
    d. Key bed

11. A _____ zone or _____ area is the interface between land and a stream. Plant communities along the river margins are called _____ vegetation, characterized by hydrophilic plants. _____ zones are significant in ecology, environmental management, and civil engineering because of their role in soil conservation, their biodiversity, and the influence they have on aquatic ecosystems.
    a. 1509 Istanbul earthquake
    b. Riparian
    c. 1703 Genroku earthquake
    d. 1700 Cascadia earthquake

12. _____ is the geological process by which material is added to a landform or land mass. Fluids such as wind and water, as well as sediment gravity flows, transport previously eroded sediment, which, at the loss of enough kinetic energy in the fluid, is deposited, building up layers of sediment.

_____ occurs when the forces responsible for sediment transportation are no longer sufficient to overcome the forces of particle weight and friction, which resist motion.

   a. Hydrothermal circulation
   b. Deposition
   c. Wave pounding
   d. Seafloor spreading

13. _____ is a naturally occurring material composed primarily of fine-grained minerals, which show plasticity through a variable range of water content, and which can be hardened when dried and/or fired. _____ deposits are mostly composed of _____ minerals (phyllosilicate minerals), minerals which impart plasticity and harden when fired and/or dried, and variable amounts of water trapped in the mineral structure by polar attraction. Organic materials which do not impart plasticity may also be a part of _____ deposits.
  a. 1703 Genroku earthquake
  b. 1700 Cascadia earthquake
  c. 1509 Istanbul earthquake
  d. Clay

14. An _____ is the result of a sudden release of energy in the Earth's crust that creates seismic waves. They are recorded with a seismometer or the related and mostly obsolete Richter magnitude, with a magnitude 3 or lower _____ being mostly imperceptible and magnitude 7 causing serious damage over large areas.
  a. AL 333
  b. AASHTO Soil Classification System
  c. AL 129-1
  d. Earthquake

15. _____ is soil composed of sand, silt, and clay in relatively even concentration (about 40-40-20% concentration respectively), considered ideal for gardening and agricultural uses. _____ soils generally contain more nutrients and humus than sandy soils, have better infiltration and drainage than silty soils, and are easier to till than clay soils.
  a. Loam
  b. 1703 Genroku earthquake
  c. 1509 Istanbul earthquake
  d. 1700 Cascadia earthquake

16. _____ is a naturally occurring granular material composed of finely divided rock and mineral particles.

As the term is used by geologists, _____ particles range in diameter from 0.0625 (or $>^1\!/_{16}$ mm, or 62.5 micrometers) to 2 millimeters. An individual particle in this range size is termed a _____ grain.

  a. Sand
  b. 1509 Istanbul earthquake
  c. 1703 Genroku earthquake
  d. 1700 Cascadia earthquake

17. _____ is soil or rock derived granular material of a grain size between sand and clay. _____ may occur as a soil or as suspended sediment in a surface water body. It may also exist as soil deposited at the bottom of a water body.
  a. Silt
  b. 1703 Genroku earthquake
  c. 1509 Istanbul earthquake
  d. 1700 Cascadia earthquake

18. In terms of soil texture, _____ usually refers to the different sizes of mineral particles in a particular sample. Soil is made up in part of finely ground rock particles, grouped according to size as sand, silt and clay. Each size plays a significantly different role.
  a. Paleosol
  b. Soil structure
  c. Mollisols
  d. Soil type

19. A _____ is a mountain rising from the ocean seafloor that does not reach to the water's surface (sea level), and thus is not an island. These are typically formed from extinct volcanoes, that rise abruptly and are usually found rising from a seafloor of 1,000-4,000 meters depth. They are defined by oceanographers as independent features that rise to at least 1,000 meters above the seafloor.
  a. 1703 Genroku earthquake
  b. 1700 Cascadia earthquake
  c. 1509 Istanbul earthquake
  d. Seamount

Chapter 11. Soil as a Resource

20. The _____ characterizes the scratch resistance of various minerals through the ability of a harder material to scratch a softer material. It was created in 1812 by the German mineralogist Friedrich Mohs and is one of several definitions of hardness in materials science. The method, however, is of great antiquity, having first been mentioned by Theophrastus in his treatise On Stones in ca 300 BC, followed by Pliny the Elder in his Naturalis Historia circa A.D.
   a. 1509 Istanbul earthquake
   b. 1700 Cascadia earthquake
   c. 1703 Genroku earthquake
   d. Mohs scale of mineral hardness

21. _____ are a soil order in USDA soil taxonomy. _____ form in semiarid to humid areas, typically under a hardwood forest cover. They have a clay-enriched subsoil and relatively high native fertility. Because of their productivity and abundance, the _____ represent one of the more important soil orders for food and fiber production. They are widely used both in agriculture and forestry and are generally easier to keep fertile than other humid-climate soils, though those in Australia and Africa are still very deficient in Nitrogen and available Phosphorus.
   a. Ultisols
   b. Entisols
   c. Illuvium
   d. Alfisols

22. A _____, sometimes called a composite volcano, is a tall, conical volcano with many layers (strata) of hardened lava, tephra, and volcanic ash. They are characterized by a steep profile and periodic, explosive eruptions. The lava that flows from a _____ tends to be viscous; it cools and hardens before spreading far.
   a. Nevado Sajama
   b. Mount Baker
   c. Stratovolcano
   d. Mount Overlord

23. _____ is the movement of the Earth's continents relative to each other. The hypothesis that continents 'drift' was first put forward by Abraham Ortelius in 1596 and was fully developed by Alfred Wegener in 1912. However, it was not until the development of the theory of plate tectonics in the 1960s, that a sufficient geological explanation of that movement was found.
   a. Continental drift
   b. Plate tectonics
   c. Thrust fault
   d. Subduction

24. In geology, _____ is transported rock debris overlying the solid bedrock. The term is also sometimes refers to organic debris so-transported. In the largest sense, it refers to the material left behind by retreating continental glaciers.
   a. Duricrust
   b. Fulgurites
   c. Gibraltar Arc
   d. Drift

25. A _____ is flat or nearly flat land adjacent to a stream or river that experiences occasional or periodic flooding. It includes the floodway, which consists of the stream channel and adjacent areas that carry flood flows, and the flood fringe, which are areas covered by the flood, but which do not experience a strong current.

They generally contain unconsolidated sediments, often extending below the bed of the stream.

   a. 1700 Cascadia earthquake
   b. 1703 Genroku earthquake
   c. Floodplain
   d. 1509 Istanbul earthquake

26. In both the FAO soil classification and the USA soil taxonomy, a _____ is a soil comprised primarily of organic materials. They are defined as having 40 centimetres (16 in) or more of organic soil material in the upper 80 centimetres (31 in.) Organic soil material has an organic carbon content (by weight) of 12 to 18 percent, or more, depending on the clay content of the soil.

a. Podsol
b. Laterite
c. Histosol
d. Vertisol

27. _____ is a surface formation in hot and wet tropical areas which is enriched in iron and aluminium and develops by intensive and long lasting weathering of the underlying parent rock. Nearly all kinds of rocks can be deeply decomposed by the action of high rainfall and elevated temperatures. The percolating rain water causes dissolution of primary rock minerals and decrease of easily soluble elements as sodium, potassium, calcium, magnesium and silicon.

   a. Soil horizon
   b. Soil structure
   c. Paleosol
   d. Laterite

28. _____ are a soil order in USA soil taxonomy. _____ form in semi-arid to semi-humid areas, typically under a grassland cover. They are most commonly found latitudinally in a band of 50 degrees north of the equator, although there are some in South America, South-Eastern Australia (mainly South Australia) and South Africa. Their parent material is generally limestone, loess, or wind-blown sand. The main processes that lead to the formation of grassland _____ are melanisation, decomposition, humification and pedoturbation.

   a. Soil horizon
   b. Paleosol
   c. Mollisols
   d. Laterite

29. _____ are an order in USDA soil taxonomy, best known for their occurrence in tropical rain forest, 15-25 degrees north and south of the Equator. Some _____ have been previously classified as laterite soils.

The main processes of soil formation of _____ are weathering, humification and pedoturbation due to animals.

   a. Ultisols
   b. Illuvium
   c. Entisols
   d. Oxisols

30. _____ consists of cutting and burning of forests or woodlands to create fields for agriculture or pasture for livestock, or for a variety of other purposes. It is sometimes part of shifting cultivation agriculture, and of transhumance livestock herding.

Historically, the practice of _____ has been widely practiced throughout most of the world, in grasslands as well as woodlands, and known by many names.

   a. 1700 Cascadia earthquake
   b. Slash and burn
   c. 1703 Genroku earthquake
   d. 1509 Istanbul earthquake

31. In soil science, _____ are the typical soils of coniferous, or Boreal forests. They are also the typical soils of eucalypt forests and heathlands in southern Australia. These soils are found in areas that are wet and cold and also in warm areas such as Florida where sandy soils have fluctuating water tables . An example of a warm-climate _____ is the Myakka fine sand, state soil of Florida.

   a. Vertisol
   b. Podsol
   c. Paleosol
   d. Soil structure

Chapter 11. Soil as a Resource

32. In both the FAO and USA soil taxonomy, a _____ is a soil in which there is a high content of expansive clay known as montmorillonite that forms deep cracks in drier seasons or years. Alternate shrinking and swelling causes self-mulching, where the soil material consistently mixes itself, causing them to have an extremely deep A horizon and no B horizon. (A soil with no B horizon is called an A/C soil).
    a. Laterite
    b. Soil horizon
    c. Soil structure
    d. Vertisol

33. A _____ is an opening in a planet's surface or crust, which allows hot, molten rock, ash, and gases to escape from below the surface. Volcanic activity involving the extrusion of rock tends to form mountains or features like mountains over a period of time.
    a. 1509 Istanbul earthquake
    b. 1700 Cascadia earthquake
    c. 1703 Genroku earthquake
    d. Volcano

34. _____ is the logging and/or burning of trees in the forested area. There are several reasons for doing so: trees or derived charcoal can be sold as a commodity and used by humans, while cleared land is used as pasture, plantations of commodities and human settlement. The removal of trees without sufficient reforestation has resulted in damage to habitat, biodiversity loss and aridity.
    a. Pacific Decadal Oscillation
    b. Greenhouse gases
    c. Glacier
    d. Deforestation

35. The _____ or the Dirty Thirties was a period of severe dust storms causing major ecological and agricultural damage to American and Canadian prairie lands from 1930 to 1936 (in some areas until 1940.) The phenomenon was caused by severe drought coupled with decades of extensive farming without crop rotation or other techniques to prevent erosion. Deep plowing of the virgin topsoil of the Great Plains had killed the natural grasses that normally kept the soil in place and trapped moisture even during periods of drought and high winds.
    a. Dust Bowl
    b. 1700 Cascadia earthquake
    c. 1509 Istanbul earthquake
    d. 1703 Genroku earthquake

36. The _____ is an informal name for the supereon comprising the eons of the geologic timescale that came before the current Phanerozoic eon. It spans from the formation of Earth around 4500 Mya (million years ago) to the evolution of abundant macroscopic hard-shelled animals, which marked the beginning of the Cambrian, the first period of the first era of the Phanerozoic eon, some 542 Mya. It is named after the Roman name for Wales - Cambria - where rocks from this age were first studied.
    a. 1700 Cascadia earthquake
    b. 1703 Genroku earthquake
    c. 1509 Istanbul earthquake
    d. Precambrian

37. _____ is the upper, outermost layer of soil, usually the top 2 inches (5.1 cm) to 8 inches (20 cm.) It has the highest concentration of organic matter and microorganisms and is where most of the Earth's biological soil activity occurs. Plants generally concentrate their roots in and obtain most of their nutrients from this layer.
    a. Topsoil
    b. Slump
    c. 1509 Istanbul earthquake
    d. Soil

38. The _____ provides a uniform system of measuring pollution levels for the major air pollutants. It is based on a scale devised by the United States Environmental Protection Agency (USEPA) to provide a way for broadcasts and newspapers to report air quality on a daily basis.

Chapter 11. Soil as a Resource

The _____ is reported as a number on a scale of 0 to 500 and is the air quality indicator.

a. 1703 Genroku earthquake
b. 1700 Cascadia earthquake
c. 1509 Istanbul earthquake
d. Pollutant Standards Index

39. _____ is any particulate matter that can be transported by fluid flow, and which eventually is deposited.

They are most often transported by water (fluvial processes) transported by wind (aeolian processes) and glaciers. Beach sands and river channel deposits are examples of fluvial transport and deposition, though _____ also often settles out of slow-moving or standing water in lakes and oceans.

a. Brickearth
b. Sediment
c. Fech fech
d. Dry quicksand

40. _____ is a type of mining in which soil and rock overlying the mineral deposit are removed. It is the opposite of underground mining, in which the overlying rock is left in place, and the mineral removed through shafts or tunnels.

_____ is used when deposits of commercially useful minerals or rock are found near the surface; that is, where the overburden (surface material covering the valuable deposit) is relatively thin or the material of interest is structurally unsuitable for tunneling (as would usually be the case for sand, cinder, and gravel.)

a. 1700 Cascadia earthquake
b. 1509 Istanbul earthquake
c. 1703 Genroku earthquake
d. Surface mining

41. _____ is the process by which soil is created. It is the major topic of the science of pedology, whose other aspects include the soil morphology, classification (taxonomy) of soils, and their distribution in nature, present and past (soil geography and paleopedology).

a. Laterite
b. Soil structure
c. Soil horizon
d. Pedogenesis

42. _____ or contour farming is the farming practice of plowing across a slope following its elevation contour lines. The rows formed have the effect of slowing water run-off during rainstorms so that the soil is not washed away and allows the water to percolate into the soil. In _____, the ruts made by the plough run perpendicular rather than parallel to slopes, generally resulting in furrows that curve around the land and are level.

a. Contour plowing
b. 1703 Genroku earthquake
c. 1509 Istanbul earthquake
d. 1700 Cascadia earthquake

43. An _____ is an underground layer of water-bearing permeable rock or unconsolidated materials (gravel, sand, silt, or clay) from which groundwater can be usefully extracted using a water well. The study of water flow in _____s and the characterization of _____s is called hydrogeology. Related terms include: an aquitard, which is an impermeable layer along an _____, and an aquiclude (or aquifuge), which is a solid, impermeable area beneath an _____.

a. AL 333
b. AL 129-1
c. Aquifer
d. AASHTO Soil Classification System

44. _____ is water located beneath the ground surface in soil pore spaces and in the fractures of lithologic formations. A unit of rock or an unconsolidated deposit is called an aquifer when it can yield a usable quantity of water. The depth at which soil pore spaces or fractures and voids in rock become completely saturated with water is called the water table.

   a. 1509 Istanbul earthquake

   b. Depression focused recharge

   c. 1700 Cascadia earthquake

   d. Groundwater

Chapter 12. Mineral and Rock Resources

1. _____, also known as open-cast mining, open-cut mining, and strip mining, refers to a method of extracting rock or minerals from the earth by their removal from an open pit or borrow.

The term is used to differentiate this form of mining from extractive methods that require tunneling into the earth. Open-pit mines are used when deposits of commercially useful minerals or rock are found near the surface; that is, where the overburden is relatively thin or the material of interest is structurally unsuitable for tunneling

    a. AL 129-1
    b. AASHTO Soil Classification System
    c. AL 333
    d. Open-pit mining

2. The _____ characterizes the scratch resistance of various minerals through the ability of a harder material to scratch a softer material. It was created in 1812 by the German mineralogist Friedrich Mohs and is one of several definitions of hardness in materials science. The method, however, is of great antiquity, having first been mentioned by Theophrastus in his treatise On Stones in ca 300 BC, followed by Pliny the Elder in his Naturalis Historia circa A.D.

    a. 1703 Genroku earthquake
    b. 1509 Istanbul earthquake
    c. 1700 Cascadia earthquake
    d. Mohs scale of mineral hardness

3. _____ is a hard, lustrous, grey metal, a chemical element with symbol Co and atomic number 27. Although _____-based colors and pigments have been used since ancient times for making jewelry and paints, and miners have long used the name kobold ore for some minerals, the free metalic _____ was not prepared and discovered until 1735 by Georg Brandt.

_____ is found in various metallic-lustred ores for example cobaltite , but it is produced as a by-product of copper and nickel mining.

    a. 1703 Genroku earthquake
    b. 1509 Istanbul earthquake
    c. 1700 Cascadia earthquake
    d. Cobalt

4. An _____ is a type of rock that contains minerals such as gemstones and metals that can be extracted through mining and refined for use. Samples of _____ in the form of exceptionally beautiful crystals, exotic layering visible when sectioned or polished or metallic presentations such as large nuggets or crystalline formations of metals such as gold or copper may command a value far beyond their value as mere _____ or raw metal for subsequent reduction to utilitarian purposes.

The grade or concentration of an _____ mineral, or metal, as well as its form of occurrence, will directly affect the costs associated with mining the _____.

    a. Ore
    b. AASHTO Soil Classification System
    c. Iron ores
    d. Ore genesis

5. _____ are rocks and minerals from which metallic iron can be economically extracted. The ores are usually rich in iron oxides and vary in color from dark grey, bright yellow, deep purple, to rusty red. The iron itself is usually found in the form of magnetite (Fe_3O_4), haematite (Fe_2O_3), goethite, limonite or siderite.

    a. Ore
    b. Iron ores
    c. AASHTO Soil Classification System
    d. Ore genesis

6. A _____ is an opening in a planet's surface or crust, which allows hot, molten rock, ash, and gases to escape from below the surface. Volcanic activity involving the extrusion of rock tends to form mountains or features like mountains over a period of time.
 a. 1703 Genroku earthquake   b. 1700 Cascadia earthquake
 c. Volcano   d. 1509 Istanbul earthquake

7. _____ is iron magnesium chromium oxide: $(Fe, Mg)Cr_2O_4$. It is an oxide mineral belonging to the spinel group. Magnesium can substitute for iron in variable amounts; also, aluminium and ferric iron commonly substitute for chromium.

_____ is found in peridotite from the Earth's mantle. It also occurs in layered ultramafic intrusive rocks. In addition, it is found in metamorphic rocks such as some serpentinites. Ore deposits of _____ form as early magmatic differentiates.

 a. Pyrope   b. 1509 Istanbul earthquake
 c. Magnesium   d. Chromite

8. _____ circulation in its most general sense is the circulation of hot water; 'hydros' in the Greek meaning water and 'thermos' meaning heat. _____ circulation occurs most often in the vicinity of sources of heat within the Earth's crust. This generally occurs near volcanic activity, but can occur in the deep crust related to the intrusion of granite, or as the result of orogeny or metamorphism.
 a. Seafloor spreading   b. Permineralization
 c. Stoping   d. Hydrothermal

9. _____ is one of the three main rock types (the others being sedimentary and metamorphic rock.) _____ is formed by magma (molten rock) being cooled and becoming solid . They may form with or without crystallization, either below the surface as intrusive (plutonic) rocks or on the surface as extrusive (volcanic) rocks. They make up approximately 95% of the upper part of the Earth's crust, but their great abundance is hidden on the Earth's surface by a relatively thin but widespread layer of sedimentary and metamorphic rocks.
 a. AL 333   b. AL 129-1
 c. AASHTO Soil Classification System   d. Igneous rock

10. _____ is a type of potassic volcanic rock best known for sometimes containing diamonds. It is named after the town of Kimberley in South Africa, where the discovery of an 83.5 carats (16.7 g) diamond in 1871 spawned a diamond rush, eventually creating the Big Hole.

_____ occurs in the Earth's crust in vertical structures known as _____ pipes.

 a. 1703 Genroku earthquake   b. 1700 Cascadia earthquake
 c. 1509 Istanbul earthquake   d. Kimberlite

11. _____ is a very coarse-grained igneous rock that has a grain size of 20 mm or more; such rocks are referred to as pegmatitic.

Most _____ is composed of quartz, feldspar and mica; in essence a 'granite'. Rarer 'intermediate' and 'mafic' _____ containing amphibole, Ca-plagioclase feldspar, pyroxene and other minerals are known, found in recrystallised zones and apophyses associated with large layered intrusions.

Chapter 12. Mineral and Rock Resources

a. Pegmatite
c. 1703 Genroku earthquake
b. 1700 Cascadia earthquake
d. 1509 Istanbul earthquake

12. A _____ is an opening in Earth's crust, often in the neighborhood of volcanoes, which emits steam and gases such as carbon dioxide, sulfur dioxide, hydrochloric acid, and hydrogen sulfide.

They may occur along tiny cracks or long fissures, in chaotic clusters or fields, and on the surfaces of lava flows and thick deposits of pyroclastic flows. A _____ field is an area of thermal springs and gas vents where magma or hot igneous rocks at shallow depth are releasing gases or interacting with groundwater.

a. 1703 Genroku earthquake
c. 1509 Istanbul earthquake
b. 1700 Cascadia earthquake
d. Fumarole

13. A _____ is a fissure in a planet's surface from which geothermally heated water issues. they are commonly found near volcanically active places, areas where tectonic plates are moving apart, ocean basins, and hotspots.

They are locally very common because the earth is both geologically active and has large amounts of water on its surface and within its crust. Common land types include hot springs, fumaroles and geysers. The most famous _____ system on land is probably within Yellowstone National Park in the United States.

a. 1703 Genroku earthquake
c. 1509 Istanbul earthquake
b. 1700 Cascadia earthquake
d. Hydrothermal vent

14. _____ are a distinctive type of rock often found in primordial sedimentary rocks. The structures consist of repeated thin layers of iron oxides, either magnetite or hematite, alternating with bands of iron-poor shale and chert. Some of the oldest known rock formations, formed around three thousand million years before present, include banded iron layers, and the banded layers are a common feature in sediments for much of the Earth's early history.

a. Banded Iron Formations
c. Jasperoid
b. Dolostone
d. Mudstone

15. A _____ or sea vent, is a type of hydrothermal vent found on the ocean floor. They are formed in fields hundreds of meters wide when superheated water from below Earth's crust comes through the ocean floor. This water is rich in dissolved minerals from the crust, most notably sulfides.

a. 1509 Istanbul earthquake
c. 1703 Genroku earthquake
b. 1700 Cascadia earthquake
d. Black smoker

16. _____ is the geological process by which material is added to a landform or land mass. Fluids such as wind and water, as well as sediment gravity flows, transport previously eroded sediment, which, at the loss of enough kinetic energy in the fluid, is deposited, building up layers of sediment.

_____ occurs when the forces responsible for sediment transportation are no longer sufficient to overcome the forces of particle weight and friction, which resist motion.

a. Wave pounding
c. Hydrothermal circulation
b. Seafloor spreading
d. Deposition

Chapter 12. Mineral and Rock Resources

17. _____ are water-soluble mineral sediments that result from the evaporation of bodies of surficial water. _____ are considered sedimentary rocks.

Although all water bodies on the surface and in aquifers contain dissolved salts, the water must evaporate into the atmosphere for the minerals to precipitate.

   a. AASHTO Soil Classification System   b. AL 129-1
   c. AL 333   d. Evaporites

18. _____ are zones, typically layers, of sediment that has been transported and deposited. They may be formed of silt and clay, sand and gravel, or large boulders. They are identical to clastic sedimentary rocks in every way except that they have not undergone diagenesis and lithification.

   a. Metasediment   b. Sandstone
   c. Keystone   d. Sedimentary deposits

19. Salt is produced by evaporation of seawater or brine from other sources, such as brine wells and salt lakes, and by mining rock salt, called halite. In 2002, total world production was estimated at 210 million tonnes, the top five producers being the United States (40.3 million tonnes), China (32.9), Germany, India (14.5), and Canada (12.3.) Note that these figures are not just for _____ but for sodium chloride in general.

The omnipresence of salt posts a problem in any coastal coating application.

   a. 1509 Istanbul earthquake   b. Table salt
   c. 1700 Cascadia earthquake   d. 1703 Genroku earthquake

20. In geology, a _____ deposit or _____ is an accumulation of valuable minerals formed by deposition of dense mineral phases in a trap site. Types of _____ deposits include alluvium, eluvium, beach _____ s, and paleoplacers.

Typical locations for alluvial _____ deposits are on the inside bends of rivers and creeks, in natural hollows, at the break of slope on a stream, the base of an escarpment, waterfall or other barrier, within sand dunes, beach profiles or in gravel beds.

   a. Placer   b. 1509 Istanbul earthquake
   c. 1700 Cascadia earthquake   d. 1703 Genroku earthquake

21. The _____ Era is one of three geologic eras of the Phanerozoic eon. The division of time into eras dates back to Giovanni Arduino, in the 18th century, although his original name for the era now called the '_____' was 'Secondary' (making the modern era the 'Tertiary'.)

The _____ was a time of tectonic, climatic and evolutionary activity. The continents gradually shifted from a state of connectedness into their present configuration; the drifting provided for speciation and other important evolutionary developments.

Chapter 12. Mineral and Rock Resources

a. 1700 Cascadia earthquake
c. Mesozoic
b. 1703 Genroku earthquake
d. 1509 Istanbul earthquake

22. The _____ was proposed by the Danish geological pioneer Nicholas Steno (1638-1686.) This principle states that layers of sediment are originally deposited horizontally. The principle is important to the analysis of folded and tilted strata.
    a. Principle of Original Horizontality
    c. Cyclostratigraphy
    b. Bedrock
    d. Key bed

23. A _____ zone or _____ area is the interface between land and a stream. Plant communities along the river margins are called _____ vegetation, characterized by hydrophilic plants. _____ zones are significant in ecology, environmental management, and civil engineering because of their role in soil conservation, their biodiversity, and the influence they have on aquatic ecosystems.
    a. Riparian
    c. 1703 Genroku earthquake
    b. 1700 Cascadia earthquake
    d. 1509 Istanbul earthquake

24. _____ is the solid-state recrystallization of pre-existing rocks due to changes in physical and chemical conditions, primarily heat, pressure, and the introduction of chemically active fluids. Both mineralogical, chemical and crystallographic changes can occur during this process.

Three types of _____ exist: dynamic, contact and regional.

    a. Lake capture
    c. Metamorphism
    b. Gibraltar Arc
    d. Pumice raft

25. _____ are type of elastic wave, also called seismic waves, that can travel through gases, elastic solids and liquids, including the Earth. _____ can be produced by earthquakes and recorded by seismometers.
    a. 1700 Cascadia earthquake
    c. 1703 Genroku earthquake
    b. 1509 Istanbul earthquake
    d. P-waves

26. An _____ is the result of a sudden release of energy in the Earth's crust that creates seismic waves. They are recorded with a seismometer or the related and mostly obsolete Richter magnitude, with a magnitude 3 or lower _____ being mostly imperceptible and magnitude 7 causing serious damage over large areas.
    a. AASHTO Soil Classification System
    c. AL 129-1
    b. Earthquake
    d. AL 333

27. _____ is rock that is of a specific particle size range. Specifically, it is any loose rock that is larger than two millimeters (2mm) in its largest dimension (about 1/12 of an inch) and no more than 64 millimeters (about 2.5 inches.) The next smaller size class in geology is sand, which is >0.0625 mm to 2 mm in size.
    a. 1700 Cascadia earthquake
    c. 1509 Istanbul earthquake
    b. Gravel
    d. 1703 Genroku earthquake

28. _____ is soil or rock derived granular material of a grain size between sand and clay. _____ may occur as a soil or as suspended sediment in a surface water body. It may also exist as soil deposited at the bottom of a water body.

Chapter 12. Mineral and Rock Resources

a. 1700 Cascadia earthquake
c. 1703 Genroku earthquake
b. 1509 Istanbul earthquake
d. Silt

29. The general term '_____' or, more precisely, 'glacial age' denotes a geological period of long-term reduction in the temperature of the Earth's surface and atmosphere, resulting in an expansion of continental ice sheets, polar ice sheets and alpine glaciers. Within a long-term _____, individual pulses of extra cold climate are termed 'glaciations'. Glaciologically, _____ implies the presence of extensive ice sheets in the northern and southern hemispheres; by this definition we are still in an _____
 a. AL 129-1
 c. AL 333
 b. AASHTO Soil Classification System
 d. Ice Age

30. A _____ is a mountain rising from the ocean seafloor that does not reach to the water's surface (sea level), and thus is not an island. These are typically formed from extinct volcanoes, that rise abruptly and are usually found rising from a seafloor of 1,000-4,000 meters depth. They are defined by oceanographers as independent features that rise to at least 1,000 meters above the seafloor.
 a. 1703 Genroku earthquake
 c. 1700 Cascadia earthquake
 b. 1509 Istanbul earthquake
 d. Seamount

31. The _____ is a tectonic spreading center located off the coasts of the state of Washington in the United States and the province of British Columbia in Canada. It runs northward from a transform boundary, the Blanco Fracture Zone, to a triple junction with the Nootka Fault and the Sovanco Fracture Zone. To its east is the Juan de Fuca Plate, which together with the Gorda Plate to its south and the Explorer Plate to its north, is what remains of the once-vast Farallon Plate which has been largely subducted under the North American Plate.
 a. Juan de Fuca ridge
 c. Forearc
 b. Thrust fault
 d. Continental crust

32. _____ is a type of mining in which soil and rock overlying the mineral deposit are removed. It is the opposite of underground mining, in which the overlying rock is left in place, and the mineral removed through shafts or tunnels.

_____ is used when deposits of commercially useful minerals or rock are found near the surface; that is, where the overburden (surface material covering the valuable deposit) is relatively thin or the material of interest is structurally unsuitable for tunneling (as would usually be the case for sand, cinder, and gravel.)
 a. 1509 Istanbul earthquake
 c. 1703 Genroku earthquake
 b. Surface mining
 d. 1700 Cascadia earthquake

33. In geology, engineering, and surveying, _____ is the motion of a surface (usually, the Earth's surface) as it shifts downward relative to a datum such as sea-level. The opposite of _____ is uplift, which results in an increase in elevation. There are several types of _____.
 a. 1509 Istanbul earthquake
 c. Subsidence
 b. Pothole
 d. 1700 Cascadia earthquake

34. _____ is the removal of solids (sediment, soil, rock and other particles) in the natural environment. It usually occurs due to transport by wind, water, or ice; by down-slope creep of soil and other material under the force of gravity; or by living organisms, such as burrowing animals, in the case of bioerosion.

_____ is distinguished from weathering, which is the process of chemical or physical breakdown of the minerals in the rocks, although the two processes may occur concurrently.

a. AASHTO Soil Classification System
b. AL 333
c. AL 129-1
d. Erosion

35. _____, otherwise known as mineral dressing, is the practice of beneficiating valuable minerals from their ores. Industrial mineral treatment processes usually combine a number of unit operations in order to liberate and separate minerals by exploiting the differences in physical properties of the different minerals that make up an ore.

Many plants also incorporate hydrometallurgical or pyrometallurgical processes as part of an extractive metallurgical operation.

a. 1703 Genroku earthquake
b. 1509 Istanbul earthquake
c. 1700 Cascadia earthquake
d. Mineral processing

36. _____ is a form of extractive metallurgy; its main use is to produce a metal from its ore. This includes iron extraction (for the production of steel) from iron ore, and copper extraction and other base metals from their ores. _____ uses heat and a chemical reducing agent, commonly a fuel that is a source of carbon such as coke, or in earlier times charcoal, to change the oxidation state of the metal ore.

a. 1703 Genroku earthquake
b. 1700 Cascadia earthquake
c. 1509 Istanbul earthquake
d. Smelting

37. _____ is the naturally occurring, unconsolidated or loose covering on the Earth's surface. _____ is composed of particles of broken rock that have been altered by chemical, biological and environmental processes including weathering and erosion. _____ is different from its parent rock(s) source(s), altered by interactions between the lithosphere, hydrosphere, atmosphere, and the biosphere.

a. Slump
b. Soil
c. 1509 Istanbul earthquake
d. Topsoil

38. _____ are the materials left over after the process of separating the valuable fraction from the worthless fraction of an ore.

_____ represent external costs of mining. As mining techniques and the price of minerals improve, it is not unusual for _____ to be reprocessed using new methods, or more thoroughly with old methods, to recover additional minerals.

a. 1509 Istanbul earthquake
b. 1700 Cascadia earthquake
c. Tailings
d. 1703 Genroku earthquake

Chapter 13. Energy Resources-Fossil Fuels

1. The _____ is a geologic fault zone capable of generating significantly destructive earthquakes. About 60 kilometers long, it lies mainly along the western base of the hills on the east side of San Francisco Bay. It runs through densely-populated areas, including the cities of Richmond, El Cerrito, Berkeley, Oakland, San Leandro, Hayward, Fremont, and San Jose.

The _____ is parallel to its more famous (and much longer) westerly neighbor, the San Andreas Fault, which lies offshore and through the San Francisco peninsula.

   a. 1703 Genroku earthquake
   b. 1700 Cascadia earthquake
   c. 1509 Istanbul earthquake
   d. Hayward Fault Zone

2. The _____ Era is one of three geologic eras of the Phanerozoic eon. The division of time into eras dates back to Giovanni Arduino, in the 18th century, although his original name for the era now called the '_____' was 'Secondary' (making the modern era the 'Tertiary'.)

The _____ was a time of tectonic, climatic and evolutionary activity. The continents gradually shifted from a state of connectedness into their present configuration; the drifting provided for speciation and other important evolutionary developments.

   a. 1703 Genroku earthquake
   b. 1700 Cascadia earthquake
   c. 1509 Istanbul earthquake
   d. Mesozoic

3. A _____ is a natural formation (or landform) where a rock arch forms, with a natural passageway through underneath. Most _____es form as a narrow ridge, walled by cliffs, become narrower from erosion, with a softer rock stratum under the cliff-forming stratum gradually eroding out until the rock shelters thus formed meet underneath the ridge, thus forming the arch. They commonly form where cliffs are subject to erosion from the sea, rivers or weathering (sub-aerial processes); the processes 'find' weaknesses in rocks and work on them, making them bigger until they break through.
   a. 1509 Istanbul earthquake
   b. 1703 Genroku earthquake
   c. 1700 Cascadia earthquake
   d. Natural arch

4. The _____ is a vast yet shallow underground water table aquifer located beneath the Great Plains in the United States. One of the world's largest aquifers, it covers an area of approximately 174,000 mi^2 in portions of the eight states of South Dakota, Nebraska, Wyoming, Colorado, Kansas, Oklahoma, New Mexico, and Texas. It was named in 1898 by N.H. Darton from its type locality near the town of Ogallala, Nebraska.
   a. AL 129-1
   b. AASHTO Soil Classification System
   c. AL 333
   d. Ogallala aquifer

5. The _____ is a classification used for most Western Hemisphere tropical cyclones that exceed the intensities of tropical depressions and tropical storms. The scale divides hurricanes into five categories distinguished by the intensities of their sustained winds. In order to be classified as a hurricane, a tropical cyclone must have maximum sustained winds of at least 74 mph (33 m/s; 64 kt; 119 km/h.)
   a. 1703 Genroku earthquake
   b. 1509 Istanbul earthquake
   c. Saffir-Simpson Hurricane Scale
   d. 1700 Cascadia earthquake

Chapter 13. Energy Resources-Fossil Fuels

6. An _____ is an underground layer of water-bearing permeable rock or unconsolidated materials (gravel, sand, silt, or clay) from which groundwater can be usefully extracted using a water well. The study of water flow in _____s and the characterization of _____s is called hydrogeology. Related terms include: an aquitard, which is an impermeable layer along an _____, and an aquiclude (or aquifuge), which is a solid, impermeable area beneath an _____.
   a. AL 129-1
   b. AL 333
   c. AASHTO Soil Classification System
   d. Aquifer

7. A _____ or sandbar is a somewhat linear landform within or extending into a body of water, typically composed of sand, silt or small pebbles. A bar is characteristically long and narrow and develops where a stream or ocean current promotes deposition of granular material, resulting in localized shallowing of the water. Bars can appear in the sea, in a lake, or in a river.

The term _____ can be applied to larger geological units that form off a coastline as part of the process of coastal erosion. These include spits and baymouth bars that form across the front of embayments and rias. A tombolo is a bar that forms an isthmus between an island or offshore rock and a mainland shore.

   a. 1700 Cascadia earthquake
   b. 1703 Genroku earthquake
   c. 1509 Istanbul earthquake
   d. Shoal

8. In geology, a _____ or _____ line is a planar fracture in rock in which the rock on one side of the fracture has moved with respect to the rock on the other side. Large _____s within the Earth's crust are the result of differential or shear motion and active _____ zones are the causal locations of most earthquakes. Earthquakes are caused by energy release during rapid slippage along a _____.
   a. Tarn
   b. Streak
   c. Stack
   d. Fault

9. _____ are the preserved remains or traces of animals, plants, and other organisms from the remote past. The totality of _____, both discovered and undiscovered, and their placement in fossiliferous rock formations and sedimentary layers (strata) is known as the fossil record. The study of _____ across geological time, how they were formed, and the evolutionary relationships between taxa (phylogeny) are some of the most important functions of the science of paleontology.
   a. 1509 Istanbul earthquake
   b. 1700 Cascadia earthquake
   c. 1703 Genroku earthquake
   d. Fossils

10. In organic chemistry, a _____ is an organic compound consisting entirely of hydrogen and carbon. With relation to chemical terminology, aromatic _____s or arenes, alkanes, alkenes and alkyne-based compounds composed entirely of carbon or hydrogen are referred to as 'pure' _____s, whereas other _____s with bonded compounds or impurities of sulfur or nitrogen, are referred to as 'impure', and remain somewhat erroneously referred to as _____s.

_____s are referred to as consisting of a 'backbone' or 'skeleton' composed entirely of carbon and hydrogen and other bonded compounds, and have a functional group that generally facilitates combustion.

   a. 1700 Cascadia earthquake
   b. Hydrocarbon
   c. 1703 Genroku earthquake
   d. 1509 Istanbul earthquake

Chapter 13. Energy Resources-Fossil Fuels

11. A _____ is a mountain rising from the ocean seafloor that does not reach to the water's surface (sea level), and thus is not an island. These are typically formed from extinct volcanoes, that rise abruptly and are usually found rising from a seafloor of 1,000-4,000 meters depth. They are defined by oceanographers as independent features that rise to at least 1,000 meters above the seafloor.
   - a. 1700 Cascadia earthquake
   - b. 1703 Genroku earthquake
   - c. 1509 Istanbul earthquake
   - d. Seamount

12. _____ is a gas consisting primarily of methane. It is found associated with fossil fuels, in coal beds, as methane clathrates, and is created by methanogenic organisms in marshes, bogs, and landfills. It is an important fuel source, a major feedstock for fertilizers, and a potent greenhouse gas.
   - a. 1703 Genroku earthquake
   - b. 1509 Istanbul earthquake
   - c. Natural gas
   - d. 1700 Cascadia earthquake

13. _____ is the consumption of energy or power. It is covered in the following articles and categories:

   - World energy resources and consumption
   - Domestic _____
   - Efficient energy use
   - Energy conservation, the practice of decreasing the quantity of energy used

   - a. AL 129-1
   - b. AASHTO Soil Classification System
   - c. Energy consumption
   - d. AL 333

14. _____ are the estimated quantities of crude oil that are claimed to be recoverable under existing economic and operating conditions.

   The total estimated amount of oil in an oil reservoir, including both producible and non-producible oil, is called oil in place. However, because of reservoir characteristics and limitations in petroleum extraction technologies only a fraction of this oil can be brought to the surface, and it is only this producible fraction that is considered to be reserves.

   - a. AASHTO Soil Classification System
   - b. AL 333
   - c. AL 129-1
   - d. Oil reserves

15. _____, meaning 'new eruption', is a volcano located on the Alaska Peninsula in Katmai National Park and Preserve, about 290 miles (470 km) southwest of Anchorage. Formed in 1912 during one of the largest volcanic eruptions of the 20th century, _____ released 30 times the volume of magma as the 1980 eruption of Mount St. Helens. Map showing volcanoes of Alaska.

   One of the largest eruptions of the 20th century occurred in 1912, from June 6 to June 8, to form _____.

   - a. 1509 Istanbul earthquake
   - b. Novarupta
   - c. 1703 Genroku earthquake
   - d. 1700 Cascadia earthquake

16. The _____ is an emergency fuel store of oil maintained by the United States Department of Energy.

The US _____ is the largest emergency supply in the world with the current capacity to hold up to 727 million barrels (1.156E+8 m^3.) The second largest emergency supply of oil is Japan's with a 2003 reported capacity of 579 million barrels .

   a. 1700 Cascadia earthquake   b. 1703 Genroku earthquake
   c. Strategic Petroleum Reserve   d. 1509 Istanbul earthquake

17. _____ is the ongoing effort to provide sufficient primary energy sources and secondary energy forms to fulfill civilization's needs. It involves both installation of established technologies and research and development to create new energy-related technologies. Major considerations in energy planning include resource depletion, supply production peaks, security of supply, cost, impact on air pollution and water pollution, and whether or not the source is renewable.

   a. Energy development   b. AL 333
   c. AASHTO Soil Classification System   d. AL 129-1

18. An _____ is a region with an abundance of oil wells extracting petroleum (crude oil) from below ground. Because the oil reservoirs typically extend over a large area, possibly several hundred kilometres across, full exploitation entails multiple wells scattered across the area. In addition, there may be exploratory wells probing the edges, pipelines to transport the oil elsewhere, and support facilities.

   a. AL 129-1   b. AL 333
   c. AASHTO Soil Classification System   d. Oil field

19. A _____ is an opening in a planet's surface or crust, which allows hot, molten rock, ash, and gases to escape from below the surface. Volcanic activity involving the extrusion of rock tends to form mountains or features like mountains over a period of time.

   a. 1700 Cascadia earthquake   b. 1703 Genroku earthquake
   c. Volcano   d. 1509 Istanbul earthquake

20. The term _____ can be used to describe both the conduct of a survey for geological purposes and an institution holding geological information.

A _____ is the systematic investigation of the subsurface of a given piece of ground for the purpose of creating a geological map or model. A _____ employs techniques from the traditional walk-over survey, studying outcrops and landforms, to intrusive methods, such as hand augering and machine driven boreholes, to the use of geophysical techniques and remote sensing methods, such as aerial photography and satellite imagery.

   a. Georeactor   b. Gradualism
   c. Geological Survey   d. Patterned ground

21. The _____ is an informal name for the supereon comprising the eons of the geologic timescale that came before the current Phanerozoic eon. It spans from the formation of Earth around 4500 Mya (million years ago) to the evolution of abundant macroscopic hard-shelled animals, which marked the beginning of the Cambrian, the first period of the first era of the Phanerozoic eon, some 542 Mya. It is named after the Roman name for Wales - Cambria - where rocks from this age were first studied.

Chapter 13. Energy Resources-Fossil Fuels

a. 1509 Istanbul earthquake
b. 1703 Genroku earthquake
c. 1700 Cascadia earthquake
d. Precambrian

22. _____ is a generic term for techniques for increasing the amount of crude oil that can be extracted from an oil field. Using _____, 30-60 %, or more, of the reservoir's original oil can be extracted compared with 20-40% using primary and secondary recovery.

_____ is also called improved oil recovery or tertiary recovery (as opposed to primary and secondary recovery.)

a. AL 333
b. AL 129-1
c. AASHTO Soil Classification System
d. Enhanced oil recovery

23. _____ are crystalline water-based solids physically resembling ice, in which small non polar molecules (typically gases) are trapped inside 'cages' of hydrogen bonded water molecules. In other words, _____ are clathrate compounds in which the host molecule is water and the guest molecule is typically a gas.

a. 1703 Genroku earthquake
b. 1700 Cascadia earthquake
c. 1509 Istanbul earthquake
d. Clathrate hydrates

24. The _____ is a chronologic schema (or idealized model) relating stratigraphy to time that is used by geologists, paleontologists and other earth scientists to describe the timing and relationships between events that have occurred during the history of the Earth. The table of geologic time spans presented here agrees with the dates and nomenclature proposed by the International Commission on Stratigraphy, and uses the standard color codes of the United States Geological Survey.

Evidence from radiometric dating indicates that the Earth is about 4.570 billion years old.

a. 1703 Genroku earthquake
b. 1700 Cascadia earthquake
c. 1509 Istanbul earthquake
d. Geologic time scale

25. _____ is a term used in inorganic chemistry and organic chemistry to indicate that a substance contains water. The chemical state of the water varies widely between _____s, some of which were so labeled before their chemical structure was understood.

In organic chemistry, a _____ is a compound formed by the addition of water or its elements to a host molecule.

a. 1509 Istanbul earthquake
b. 1703 Genroku earthquake
c. Hydrate
d. 1700 Cascadia earthquake

26. _____ is soil or rock derived granular material of a grain size between sand and clay. _____ may occur as a soil or as suspended sediment in a surface water body. It may also exist as soil deposited at the bottom of a water body.

a. 1703 Genroku earthquake
b. Silt
c. 1700 Cascadia earthquake
d. 1509 Istanbul earthquake

Chapter 13. Energy Resources-Fossil Fuels

27. The general term '_____' or, more precisely, 'glacial age' denotes a geological period of long-term reduction in the temperature of the Earth's surface and atmosphere, resulting in an expansion of continental ice sheets, polar ice sheets and alpine glaciers. Within a long-term _____, individual pulses of extra cold climate are termed 'glaciations'. Glaciologically, _____ implies the presence of extensive ice sheets in the northern and southern hemispheres; by this definition we are still in an _____
   a. AL 129-1
   b. AL 333
   c. AASHTO Soil Classification System
   d. Ice Age

28. _____ is a hard, compact variety of mineral coal that has a high lustre. It has the highest carbon count and contains the fewest impurities of all coals, despite its lower calorific content.

   _____ is the highest of the metamorphic rank, in which the carbon content is between 92% and 98%.

   a. Anthracite
   b. AASHTO Soil Classification System
   c. AL 333
   d. AL 129-1

29. _____ is a relatively soft coal containing a tarlike substance called bitumen. It is of higher quality than lignite coal but of poorer quality than anthracite coal.

   _____ is a sedimorphic rock formed by diagenetic and submetamorphic compression of peat bog material.

   a. 1700 Cascadia earthquake
   b. 1509 Istanbul earthquake
   c. 1703 Genroku earthquake
   d. Bituminous coal

30. _____ is an accumulation of partially decayed vegetation matter. _____ forms in wetlands or peatlands, variously called bogs, moors, muskegs, pocosins, mires, and _____ swamp forests. By volume there are about 4 trillion mÂ³ of _____ in the world covering a total of around 2% of global land mass (about 3 million km^2), containing about 8 billion terajoules of energy.
   a. 1703 Genroku earthquake
   b. 1700 Cascadia earthquake
   c. 1509 Istanbul earthquake
   d. Peat

31. _____ is a process that converts carbonaceous materials, such as coal, petroleum, biofuel into carbon monoxide and hydrogen by reacting the raw material at high temperatures with a controlled amount of oxygen and/or steam. The resulting gas mixture is called synthesis gas or syngas and is itself a fuel. _____ is a method for extracting energy from many different types of organic materials.
   a. 1509 Istanbul earthquake
   b. 1700 Cascadia earthquake
   c. 1703 Genroku earthquake
   d. Gasification

32. The _____ characterizes the scratch resistance of various minerals through the ability of a harder material to scratch a softer material. It was created in 1812 by the German mineralogist Friedrich Mohs and is one of several definitions of hardness in materials science. The method, however, is of great antiquity, having first been mentioned by Theophrastus in his treatise On Stones in ca 300 BC, followed by Pliny the Elder in his Naturalis Historia circa A.D.
   a. 1700 Cascadia earthquake
   b. 1703 Genroku earthquake
   c. 1509 Istanbul earthquake
   d. Mohs scale of mineral hardness

Chapter 13. Energy Resources-Fossil Fuels

33. _____ is a type of mining in which soil and rock overlying the mineral deposit are removed. It is the opposite of underground mining, in which the overlying rock is left in place, and the mineral removed through shafts or tunnels.

_____ is used when deposits of commercially useful minerals or rock are found near the surface; that is, where the overburden (surface material covering the valuable deposit) is relatively thin or the material of interest is structurally unsuitable for tunneling (as would usually be the case for sand, cinder, and gravel.)

  a. 1703 Genroku earthquake   b. Surface mining
  c. 1700 Cascadia earthquake   d. 1509 Istanbul earthquake

34. _____ is the chemical compound with the formula SO_2. It is produced by volcanoes and in various industrial processes. Since coal and petroleum often contain sulfur compounds, their combustion generates _____.

  a. 1703 Genroku earthquake   b. 1700 Cascadia earthquake
  c. 1509 Istanbul earthquake   d. Sulfur dioxide

35. _____ are type of elastic wave, also called seismic waves, that can travel through gases, elastic solids and liquids, including the Earth. _____ can be produced by earthquakes and recorded by seismometers.

  a. 1509 Istanbul earthquake   b. 1700 Cascadia earthquake
  c. 1703 Genroku earthquake   d. P-waves

36. _____ is the process of creating useful landscapes that meet a variety of goals, typically creating productive ecosystems (or sometimes industrial or municipal land) from mined land. It includes all aspects of this work, including material placement, stabilizing, capping, regrading, placing cover soils, revegetation, and maintenance.

In the USA, _____ is a regular part of modern mining practice.

  a. Mine reclamation   b. 1700 Cascadia earthquake
  c. 1509 Istanbul earthquake   d. 1703 Genroku earthquake

37. The _____ is an Eocene geologic formation that records the sedimentation in a series of intermountain lakes. The sedimentary layers were formed in a large area of interconnecting lakes a tributary of the Colorado River. The area of the formation exists as three separate basins around the Uinta Mountains of northeastern Utah: an area in northwestern Colorado east of the Uintas, a larger area in the southwest corner of Wyoming just north of the Uintas known as Lake Gosiute, and the largest area, which lies in northeastern Utah and western Colorado south of the Uintas, known as Lake Uinta.

  a. 1509 Istanbul earthquake   b. 1703 Genroku earthquake
  c. 1700 Cascadia earthquake   d. Green River Formation

38. _____ is a mixture of organic chemical compounds that make up a portion of the organic matter in sedimentary rocks. It is insoluble in normal organic solvents because of the huge molecular weight (upwards of 1,000 Daltons) of its component compounds. The soluble portion is known as bitumen.

  a. 1703 Genroku earthquake   b. 1509 Istanbul earthquake
  c. 1700 Cascadia earthquake   d. Kerogen

Chapter 13. Energy Resources-Fossil Fuels

39. _____ is an organic-rich fine-grained sedimentary rock. It contains significant amounts of kerogen, a solid mixture of organic chemical compounds from which liquid hydrocarbons can be extracted. Deposits of _____ occur around the world, including major deposits in the United States of America. Estimates of global deposits range from 2.8 trillion to 3.3 trillion barrels >(450 >× 10^9 to 520 >× 10^9 m^3) of recoverable oil.
    a. AL 129-1   b. AL 333
    c. AASHTO Soil Classification System   d. Oil shale

40. _____ is a fine-grained sedimentary rock whose original constituents were clay minerals or muds. It is characterized by thin laminae breaking with an irregular curving fracture, often splintery and usually parallel to the often-indistinguishable bedding plane. This property is called fissility.
    a. Dolomite   b. Shale
    c. Mudstone   d. Porcellanite

41. _____ is the naturally occurring, unconsolidated or loose covering on the Earth's surface. _____ is composed of particles of broken rock that have been altered by chemical, biological and environmental processes including weathering and erosion. _____ is different from its parent rock(s) source(s), altered by interactions between the lithosphere, hydrosphere, atmosphere, and the biosphere.
    a. Slump   b. Soil
    c. 1509 Istanbul earthquake   d. Topsoil

42. _____ is a naturally occurring granular material composed of finely divided rock and mineral particles.

As the term is used by geologists, _____ particles range in diameter from 0.0625 (or >^{1}>⁄$_{16}$ mm, or 62.5 micrometers) to 2 millimeters. An individual particle in this range size is termed a _____ grain.

    a. 1509 Istanbul earthquake   b. 1700 Cascadia earthquake
    c. Sand   d. 1703 Genroku earthquake

43. _____ or extra heavy oil, is a type of bitumen deposit. The sands are naturally occurring mixtures of sand or clay, water and an extremely dense and viscous form of petroleum called bitumen. They are found in large amounts in many countries throughout the world, but are found in extremely large quantities in Canada and Venezuela.
    a. AL 129-1   b. Oil sands
    c. AL 333   d. AASHTO Soil Classification System

44. _____, also known as open-cast mining, open-cut mining, and strip mining, refers to a method of extracting rock or minerals from the earth by their removal from an open pit or borrow.

The term is used to differentiate this form of mining from extractive methods that require tunneling into the earth. Open-pit mines are used when deposits of commercially useful minerals or rock are found near the surface; that is, where the overburden is relatively thin or the material of interest is structurally unsuitable for tunneling

    a. AL 129-1   b. AL 333
    c. AASHTO Soil Classification System   d. Open-pit mining

Chapter 14. Energy Resources-Alternative Sources

1. In geology, _____ refers to heat sources within the planet. _____ is technically an adjective (e.g., _____ energy) but in U.S. English the word has attained frequent use as a noun.

The planet's internal heat was originally generated during its accretion, due to gravitational binding energy, and since then additional heat has continued to be generated by decay heat from the radioactive decay of elements.

- a. Fault
- b. Diamond Head
- c. Platform
- d. Geothermal

2. _____ is power extracted from heat stored in the earth. This geothermal energy originates from the original formation of the planet, from radioactive decay of minerals, and from solar energy absorbed at the surface. It has been used for space heating and bathing since ancient roman times, but is now better known for generating electricity.
- a. Geothermal desalination
- b. Geothermal power
- c. Hot Dry Rock Geothermal Energy
- d. Geothermal gradient

3. A _____ or sandbar is a somewhat linear landform within or extending into a body of water, typically composed of sand, silt or small pebbles. A bar is characteristically long and narrow and develops where a stream or ocean current promotes deposition of granular material, resulting in localized shallowing of the water. Bars can appear in the sea, in a lake, or in a river.

The term _____ can be applied to larger geological units that form off a coastline as part of the process of coastal erosion. These include spits and baymouth bars that form across the front of embayments and rias. A tombolo is a bar that forms an isthmus between an island or offshore rock and a mainland shore.

- a. 1703 Genroku earthquake
- b. Shoal
- c. 1509 Istanbul earthquake
- d. 1700 Cascadia earthquake

4. _____ is the consumption of energy or power. It is covered in the following articles and categories:

- World energy resources and consumption
- Domestic _____
- Efficient energy use
- Energy conservation, the practice of decreasing the quantity of energy used

- a. AL 333
- b. AL 129-1
- c. AASHTO Soil Classification System
- d. Energy consumption

5. _____ are the preserved remains or traces of animals, plants, and other organisms from the remote past. The totality of _____, both discovered and undiscovered, and their placement in fossiliferous rock formations and sedimentary layers (strata) is known as the fossil record. The study of _____ across geological time, how they were formed, and the evolutionary relationships between taxa (phylogeny) are some of the most important functions of the science of paleontology.
- a. 1700 Cascadia earthquake
- b. 1703 Genroku earthquake
- c. 1509 Istanbul earthquake
- d. Fossils

Chapter 14. Energy Resources-Alternative Sources

6. A _____ is a mountain rising from the ocean seafloor that does not reach to the water's surface (sea level), and thus is not an island. These are typically formed from extinct volcanoes, that rise abruptly and are usually found rising from a seafloor of 1,000-4,000 meters depth. They are defined by oceanographers as independent features that rise to at least 1,000 meters above the seafloor.
    a. Seamount
    b. 1703 Genroku earthquake
    c. 1700 Cascadia earthquake
    d. 1509 Istanbul earthquake

7. In physics, _____ is the rate at which work is performed or energy is transmitted, or the amount of energy required or expended for a given unit of time. As a rate of change of work done or the energy of a subsystem, _____ is:

$$P = \frac{W}{t}$$

where P is _____, W is work and t is time.

The average _____ (often simply called '_____' when the context makes it clear) is the average amount of work done or energy transferred per unit time.

    a. 1700 Cascadia earthquake
    b. Power
    c. 1509 Istanbul earthquake
    d. 1703 Genroku earthquake

8. An _____ is the result of a sudden release of energy in the Earth's crust that creates seismic waves. They are recorded with a seismometer or the related and mostly obsolete Richter magnitude, with a magnitude 3 or lower _____ being mostly imperceptible and magnitude 7 causing serious damage over large areas.
    a. AL 129-1
    b. AL 333
    c. AASHTO Soil Classification System
    d. Earthquake

9. The _____ is the epoch from 1.8 million to 11550 years BP covering the world's recent period of repeated glaciations. The _____ epoch follows the Pliocene epoch and is followed by the Holocene epoch. The _____ is the third epoch of the Neogene period or 6th epoch of the Cenozoic Era. The end of the _____ corresponds with the retreat of the last continental glacier. It also corresponds with the end of the Paleolithic age used in archaeology.
    a. Sicilian Stage
    b. Tyrrhenian
    c. Pleistocene
    d. Late Pleistocene

10. _____, also known as the Pleistocene glaciation, the current ice age or simply the ice age, refers to the period of the last few million years in which permanent ice sheets were established in Antarctica and perhaps Greenland, and fluctuating ice sheets have occurred elsewhere The major effects of the ice age were erosion and deposition of material over large parts of the continents, modification of river systems, creation of millions of lakes, changes in sea level, development of pluvial lakes far from the ice margins, isostatic adjustment of the crust, and abnormal winds. It affected oceans, flooding, and biological communities.
    a. Glacial period
    b. Quaternary glaciation
    c. Bergschrund
    d. Wolstonian Stage

11. The _____ was proposed by the Danish geological pioneer Nicholas Steno (1638-1686.) This principle states that layers of sediment are originally deposited horizontally. The principle is important to the analysis of folded and tilted strata.

Chapter 14. Energy Resources-Alternative Sources

a. Key bed
b. Cyclostratigraphy
c. Bedrock
d. Principle of Original Horizontality

12. The _____ is a geologic fault zone capable of generating significantly destructive earthquakes. About 60 kilometers long, it lies mainly along the western base of the hills on the east side of San Francisco Bay. It runs through densely-populated areas, including the cities of Richmond, El Cerrito, Berkeley, Oakland, San Leandro, Hayward, Fremont, and San Jose.

The _____ is parallel to its more famous (and much longer) westerly neighbor, the San Andreas Fault, which lies offshore and through the San Francisco peninsula.

a. 1700 Cascadia earthquake
b. 1509 Istanbul earthquake
c. 1703 Genroku earthquake
d. Hayward Fault Zone

13. _____, also called heavy hydrogen, is a stable isotope of hydrogen with a natural abundance in the oceans of Earth of approximately one atom in 6500 of hydrogen (~154 PPM.) _____ thus accounts for approximately 0.015% (alternately, on a weight basis: 0.030%) of all naturally occurring hydrogen in the oceans on Earth _____ abundance on Jupiter is about 2.25×10^{-5} (about 22 atoms in 1,000,000 or 15% of the terrestrial _____-to-hydrogen ratio); these ratios presumably reflect the early solar nebula ratios, and those after the Big Bang.

a. 1509 Istanbul earthquake
b. 1700 Cascadia earthquake
c. 1703 Genroku earthquake
d. Deuterium

14. In geology, a _____ or _____ line is a planar fracture in rock in which the rock on one side of the fracture has moved with respect to the rock on the other side. Large _____s within the Earth's crust are the result of differential or shear motion and active _____ zones are the causal locations of most earthquakes. Earthquakes are caused by energy release during rapid slippage along a _____.

a. Stack
b. Streak
c. Tarn
d. Fault

15. _____ is a radioactive isotope of hydrogen. The nucleus of _____ contains one proton and two neutrons, whereas the nucleus of protium (the most abundant hydrogen isotope) contains one proton and no neutrons.

While _____ has several different experimentally-determined values of its half-life, the NIST recommends 4,500±8 days (approximately 12.33 years.)

a. 1703 Genroku earthquake
b. 1700 Cascadia earthquake
c. Tritium
d. 1509 Istanbul earthquake

16. The _____ or the Dirty Thirties was a period of severe dust storms causing major ecological and agricultural damage to American and Canadian prairie lands from 1930 to 1936 (in some areas until 1940.) The phenomenon was caused by severe drought coupled with decades of extensive farming without crop rotation or other techniques to prevent erosion. Deep plowing of the virgin topsoil of the Great Plains had killed the natural grasses that normally kept the soil in place and trapped moisture even during periods of drought and high winds.

a. 1509 Istanbul earthquake
b. Dust Bowl
c. 1703 Genroku earthquake
d. 1700 Cascadia earthquake

17. A _____ is a natural formation (or landform) where a rock arch forms, with a natural passageway through underneath. Most _____es form as a narrow ridge, walled by cliffs, become narrower from erosion, with a softer rock stratum under the cliff-forming stratum gradually eroding out until the rock shelters thus formed meet underneath the ridge, thus forming the arch. They commonly form where cliffs are subject to erosion from the sea, rivers or weathering (sub-aerial processes); the processes 'find' weaknesses in rocks and work on them, making them bigger until they break through.
   a. 1703 Genroku earthquake
   b. Natural arch
   c. 1509 Istanbul earthquake
   d. 1700 Cascadia earthquake

18. _____ is a large 13 kilometres wide caldera situated to the west of Naples, Italy declared regional park in 2003. Today mostly lying underwater, the area comprises 24 craters and volcanic edifices, some of which present hydrothermal activity at Lucrino, Agnano and the town of Pozzuoli and effusive gaseous manifestations like the Solfatara crater, mythological home of the Roman god of fire, Vulcan. The area also features bradyseismic phenomena, which are most evident at the temple of Serapis in Pozzuoli.
   a. Campi Flegrei
   b. 1703 Genroku earthquake
   c. 1700 Cascadia earthquake
   d. 1509 Istanbul earthquake

19. The _____ is a chronologic schema (or idealized model) relating stratigraphy to time that is used by geologists, paleontologists and other earth scientists to describe the timing and relationships between events that have occurred during the history of the Earth. The table of geologic time spans presented here agrees with the dates and nomenclature proposed by the International Commission on Stratigraphy, and uses the standard color codes of the United States Geological Survey.

Evidence from radiometric dating indicates that the Earth is about 4.570 billion years old.

   a. 1703 Genroku earthquake
   b. Geologic time scale
   c. 1509 Istanbul earthquake
   d. 1700 Cascadia earthquake

20. _____ is water located beneath the ground surface in soil pore spaces and in the fractures of lithologic formations. A unit of rock or an unconsolidated deposit is called an aquifer when it can yield a usable quantity of water. The depth at which soil pore spaces or fractures and voids in rock become completely saturated with water is called the water table.
   a. 1700 Cascadia earthquake
   b. Groundwater
   c. Depression focused recharge
   d. 1509 Istanbul earthquake

21. In geology, engineering, and surveying, _____ is the motion of a surface (usually, the Earth's surface) as it shifts downward relative to a datum such as sea-level. The opposite of _____ is uplift, which results in an increase in elevation. There are several types of _____.
   a. 1509 Istanbul earthquake
   b. 1700 Cascadia earthquake
   c. Subsidence
   d. Pothole

22. The _____ are a volcanic group of mountains in New Mexico, United States. The highest point in the range is Chicoma Mountain (also spelled as Tschicoma or Tchicoma) at an elevation of 11,561 feet (3524 meters).

The _____ are a classic example of intracontinental volcanism and consist of a broadly circular ridge surrounding the famous Valles Caldera. The most recent known eruption was a basalt flow dated to 50,000 to 60,000 years before the present; however, most of the volume of the range is composed of rhyolite. The two most recent caldera-forming eruptions, dated to about 1.4 million and 1.1 million years ago, produced massive ignimbrite deposits known as the Otowi and Tshirege members,

- a. 1703 Genroku earthquake
- b. 1700 Cascadia earthquake
- c. 1509 Istanbul earthquake
- d. Jemez Mountains

23. _____, hydraulic power or water power is power that is derived from the force or energy of moving water, which may be harnessed for useful purposes.

Prior to the widespread availability of commercial electric power, _____ was used for irrigation, and operation of various machines, such as watermills, textile machines, sawmills, dock cranes, and domestic lifts.

Another method used a trompe, which produces compressed air from falling water, which could then be used to power other machinery at a distance from the water.

- a. 1703 Genroku earthquake
- b. 1700 Cascadia earthquake
- c. 1509 Istanbul earthquake
- d. Hydropower

24. _____ is a gas consisting primarily of methane. It is found associated with fossil fuels, in coal beds, as methane clathrates, and is created by methanogenic organisms in marshes, bogs, and landfills. It is an important fuel source, a major feedstock for fertilizers, and a potent greenhouse gas.
- a. 1700 Cascadia earthquake
- b. 1703 Genroku earthquake
- c. 1509 Istanbul earthquake
- d. Natural gas

25. The _____ is a classification used for most Western Hemisphere tropical cyclones that exceed the intensities of tropical depressions and tropical storms. The scale divides hurricanes into five categories distinguished by the intensities of their sustained winds. In order to be classified as a hurricane, a tropical cyclone must have maximum sustained winds of at least 74 mph (33 m/s; 64 kt; 119 km/h.)
- a. 1509 Istanbul earthquake
- b. 1703 Genroku earthquake
- c. 1700 Cascadia earthquake
- d. Saffir-Simpson Hurricane Scale

26. A _____ describes one of a number of pieces of legislation relating to the reduction of smog and air pollution in general. The use by governments to enforce clean air standards has contributed to an improvement in human health and longer life spans. Critics argue it has also sapped corporate profits and contributed to outsourcing, while defenders counter that improved environmental air quality has generated more jobs than it has eliminated.
- a. 1703 Genroku earthquake
- b. 1700 Cascadia earthquake
- c. 1509 Istanbul earthquake
- d. Clean Air Act

27. _____ is a process that converts carbonaceous materials, such as coal, petroleum, biofuel into carbon monoxide and hydrogen by reacting the raw material at high temperatures with a controlled amount of oxygen and/or steam. The resulting gas mixture is called synthesis gas or syngas and is itself a fuel. _____ is a method for extracting energy from many different types of organic materials.

a. 1509 Istanbul earthquake
b. 1703 Genroku earthquake
c. 1700 Cascadia earthquake
d. Gasification

28. The _____ Era is one of three geologic eras of the Phanerozoic eon. The division of time into eras dates back to Giovanni Arduino, in the 18th century, although his original name for the era now called the '_____' was 'Secondary' (making the modern era the 'Tertiary'.)

The _____ was a time of tectonic, climatic and evolutionary activity. The continents gradually shifted from a state of connectedness into their present configuration; the drifting provided for speciation and other important evolutionary developments.

a. 1700 Cascadia earthquake
b. 1703 Genroku earthquake
c. Mesozoic
d. 1509 Istanbul earthquake

29. _____ typically refers to a gas produced by the biological breakdown of organic matter in the absence of oxygen. _____ originates from biogenic material and is a type of biofuel.

One type of _____ is produced by anaerobic digestion or fermentation of biodegradable materials such as biomass, manure or sewage, municipal waste, green waste and energy crops.

a. 1509 Istanbul earthquake
b. Leachate
c. 1700 Cascadia earthquake
d. Biogas

Chapter 15. Waste Disposal

1. The _____ characterizes the scratch resistance of various minerals through the ability of a harder material to scratch a softer material. It was created in 1812 by the German mineralogist Friedrich Mohs and is one of several definitions of hardness in materials science. The method, however, is of great antiquity, having first been mentioned by Theophrastus in his treatise On Stones in ca 300 BC, followed by Pliny the Elder in his Naturalis Historia circa A.D.
   a. 1509 Istanbul earthquake
   b. 1700 Cascadia earthquake
   c. 1703 Genroku earthquake
   d. Mohs scale of mineral hardness

2. _____ is the movement of the Earth's continents relative to each other. The hypothesis that continents 'drift' was first put forward by Abraham Ortelius in 1596 and was fully developed by Alfred Wegener in 1912. However, it was not until the development of the theory of plate tectonics in the 1960s, that a sufficient geological explanation of that movement was found.
   a. Continental drift
   b. Plate tectonics
   c. Thrust fault
   d. Subduction

3. In geology, _____ is transported rock debris overlying the solid bedrock. The term is also sometimes refers to organic debris so-transported. In the largest sense, it refers to the material left behind by retreating continental glaciers.
   a. Fulgurites
   b. Duricrust
   c. Drift
   d. Gibraltar Arc

4. _____ is the removal of solids (sediment, soil, rock and other particles) in the natural environment. It usually occurs due to transport by wind, water, or ice; by down-slope creep of soil and other material under the force of gravity; or by living organisms, such as burrowing animals, in the case of bioerosion.

   _____ is distinguished from weathering, which is the process of chemical or physical breakdown of the minerals in the rocks, although the two processes may occur concurrently.

   a. AASHTO Soil Classification System
   b. Erosion
   c. AL 333
   d. AL 129-1

5. _____ is the naturally occurring, unconsolidated or loose covering on the Earth's surface. _____ is composed of particles of broken rock that have been altered by chemical, biological and environmental processes including weathering and erosion. _____ is different from its parent rock(s) source(s), altered by interactions between the lithosphere, hydrosphere, atmosphere, and the biosphere.
   a. 1509 Istanbul earthquake
   b. Slump
   c. Topsoil
   d. Soil

6. A _____ is an opening in a planet's surface or crust, which allows hot, molten rock, ash, and gases to escape from below the surface. Volcanic activity involving the extrusion of rock tends to form mountains or features like mountains over a period of time.
   a. 1700 Cascadia earthquake
   b. 1509 Istanbul earthquake
   c. 1703 Genroku earthquake
   d. Volcano

7. The _____ Era is one of three geologic eras of the Phanerozoic eon. The division of time into eras dates back to Giovanni Arduino, in the 18th century, although his original name for the era now called the '_____' was 'Secondary' (making the modern era the 'Tertiary'.)

The _____ was a time of tectonic, climatic and evolutionary activity. The continents gradually shifted from a state of connectedness into their present configuration; the drifting provided for speciation and other important evolutionary developments.

a. 1509 Istanbul earthquake
b. 1700 Cascadia earthquake
c. Mesozoic
d. 1703 Genroku earthquake

8. The _____ provides a uniform system of measuring pollution levels for the major air pollutants. It is based on a scale devised by the United States Environmental Protection Agency (USEPA) to provide a way for broadcasts and newspapers to report air quality on a daily basis.

The _____ is reported as a number on a scale of 0 to 500 and is the air quality indicator.

a. 1509 Istanbul earthquake
b. 1700 Cascadia earthquake
c. 1703 Genroku earthquake
d. Pollutant Standards Index

9. _____ is water located beneath the ground surface in soil pore spaces and in the fractures of lithologic formations. A unit of rock or an unconsolidated deposit is called an aquifer when it can yield a usable quantity of water. The depth at which soil pore spaces or fractures and voids in rock become completely saturated with water is called the water table.

a. 1700 Cascadia earthquake
b. Groundwater
c. 1509 Istanbul earthquake
d. Depression focused recharge

10. _____ is the liquid that drains or 'leaches' from a landfill; it varies widely in composition regarding the age of the landfill and the type of waste that it contains. It can usually contain both dissolved and suspended material.

The generation of _____ is caused principally by precipitation percolating through waste deposited in a landfill.

a. Biogas
b. Leachate
c. 1509 Istanbul earthquake
d. 1700 Cascadia earthquake

11. A _____ is flat or nearly flat land adjacent to a stream or river that experiences occasional or periodic flooding. It includes the floodway, which consists of the stream channel and adjacent areas that carry flood flows, and the flood fringe, which are areas covered by the flood, but which do not experience a strong current.

They generally contain unconsolidated sediments, often extending below the bed of the stream.

a. 1509 Istanbul earthquake
b. 1703 Genroku earthquake
c. Floodplain
d. 1700 Cascadia earthquake

12. _____ are the preserved remains or traces of animals, plants, and other organisms from the remote past. The totality of _____, both discovered and undiscovered, and their placement in fossiliferous rock formations and sedimentary layers (strata) is known as the fossil record. The study of _____ across geological time, how they were formed, and the evolutionary relationships between taxa (phylogeny) are some of the most important functions of the science of paleontology.

a. Fossils
c. 1509 Istanbul earthquake
b. 1700 Cascadia earthquake
d. 1703 Genroku earthquake

13. In geology, _____ refers to heat sources within the planet. _____ is technically an adjective (e.g., _____ energy) but in U.S. English the word has attained frequent use as a noun .

The planet's internal heat was originally generated during its accretion, due to gravitational binding energy, and since then additional heat has continued to be generated by decay heat from the radioactive decay of elements.

a. Fault
c. Platform
b. Geothermal
d. Diamond Head

14. _____ is power extracted from heat stored in the earth. This geothermal energy originates from the original formation of the planet, from radioactive decay of minerals, and from solar energy absorbed at the surface. It has been used for space heating and bathing since ancient roman times, but is now better known for generating electricity.

a. Geothermal gradient
c. Geothermal desalination
b. Hot Dry Rock Geothermal Energy
d. Geothermal power

15. _____ is a gas consisting primarily of methane. It is found associated with fossil fuels, in coal beds, as methane clathrates, and is created by methanogenic organisms in marshes, bogs, and landfills. It is an important fuel source, a major feedstock for fertilizers, and a potent greenhouse gas.

a. 1700 Cascadia earthquake
c. Natural gas
b. 1509 Istanbul earthquake
d. 1703 Genroku earthquake

16. The _____ is the world's third deep geological repository licensed to permanently dispose of transuranic radioactive waste for 10000 years that is left from the research and production of nuclear weapons and nuclear power plants. It is located approximately 26 miles east of Carlsbad, New Mexico, in eastern Eddy County.

a. 1700 Cascadia earthquake
c. 1703 Genroku earthquake
b. 1509 Istanbul earthquake
d. Waste Isolation Pilot Plant

17. The _____ is the epoch from 1.8 million to 11550 years BP covering the world's recent period of repeated glaciations. The _____ epoch follows the Pliocene epoch and is followed by the Holocene epoch. The _____ is the third epoch of the Neogene period or 6th epoch of the Cenozoic Era. The end of the _____ corresponds with the retreat of the last continental glacier. It also corresponds with the end of the Paleolithic age used in archaeology.

a. Sicilian Stage
c. Tyrrhenian
b. Late Pleistocene
d. Pleistocene

18. _____, also known as the Pleistocene glaciation, the current ice age or simply the ice age, refers to the period of the last few million years in which permanent ice sheets were established in Antarctica and perhaps Greenland, and fluctuating ice sheets have occurred elsewhere The major effects of the ice age were erosion and deposition of material over large parts of the continents, modification of river systems, creation of millions of lakes, changes in sea level, development of pluvial lakes far from the ice margins, isostatic adjustment of the crust, and abnormal winds. It affected oceans, flooding, and biological communities.

a. Bergschrund
c. Wolstonian Stage
b. Glacial period
d. Quaternary glaciation

19. _____ was the supercontinent that is theorized to have existed during the Paleozoic and Mesozoic eras about 250 million years ago, before the component continents were separated into their current configuration.

The name was first used by the German originator of the continental drift theory, Alfred Wegener, in the 1920 edition of his book The Origin of Continents and Oceans , in which a postulated supercontinent _____ played a key role.

The single enormous ocean which surrounded Pangaea is known as Panthalassa.

- a. 1509 Istanbul earthquake
- b. 1703 Genroku earthquake
- c. 1700 Cascadia earthquake
- d. Pangea

20. The _____ is a vast yet shallow underground water table aquifer located beneath the Great Plains in the United States. One of the world's largest aquifers, it covers an area of approximately 174,000 mi^2 in portions of the eight states of South Dakota, Nebraska, Wyoming, Colorado, Kansas, Oklahoma, New Mexico, and Texas. It was named in 1898 by N.H. Darton from its type locality near the town of Ogallala, Nebraska.
- a. AL 333
- b. Ogallala aquifer
- c. AL 129-1
- d. AASHTO Soil Classification System

21. An _____ is an underground layer of water-bearing permeable rock or unconsolidated materials (gravel, sand, silt, or clay) from which groundwater can be usefully extracted using a water well. The study of water flow in _____s and the characterization of _____s is called hydrogeology. Related terms include: an aquitard, which is an impermeable layer along an _____, and an aquiclude (or aquifuge), which is a solid, impermeable area beneath an _____.
- a. AL 129-1
- b. AASHTO Soil Classification System
- c. Aquifer
- d. AL 333

22. _____ is a clear water-insoluble liquid with the typical smell of paint thinners, redolent of the sweet smell of the related compound benzene. It is an aromatic hydrocarbon that is widely used as an industrial feedstock and as a solvent. Like other solvents, _____ is also used as an inhalant drug for its intoxicating properties.
- a. 1703 Genroku earthquake
- b. 1509 Istanbul earthquake
- c. Toluene
- d. 1700 Cascadia earthquake

23. _____ is the organic compound with the formula $CH_2{:}CHCl$. This colourless compound is an important industrial chemical chiefly used to produce the polymer polyvinyl chloride (Pvinyl chloride.) At room temperature, _____ is a gas with a sickly sweet odor that is easily condensed.
- a. Vinyl chloride
- b. 1703 Genroku earthquake
- c. 1700 Cascadia earthquake
- d. 1509 Istanbul earthquake

24. _____ is soil or rock derived granular material of a grain size between sand and clay. _____ may occur as a soil or as suspended sediment in a surface water body. It may also exist as soil deposited at the bottom of a water body.
- a. Silt
- b. 1509 Istanbul earthquake
- c. 1703 Genroku earthquake
- d. 1700 Cascadia earthquake

Chapter 15. Waste Disposal

25. _____ is the residual semi-solid material left from industrial, or wastewater treatment processes. When fresh sewage or wastewater is added to a settling tank, approximately 50% of the suspended solid matter will settle out in an hour and a half. This collection of solids is known as raw _____ or primary solids and is said to be 'fresh' before anaerobic processes become active.
   a. 1703 Genroku earthquake
   b. Sludge
   c. 1509 Istanbul earthquake
   d. 1700 Cascadia earthquake

26. _____ are high-energy, high-speed electrons or positrons emitted by certain types of radioactive nuclei such as potassium-40. The _____ emitted are a form of ionizing radiation also known as beta rays. The production of _____ is termed beta decay.
   a. 1703 Genroku earthquake
   b. 1509 Istanbul earthquake
   c. 1700 Cascadia earthquake
   d. Beta particles

27. _____ are electromagnetic radiation of high energy. They are produced by sub-atomic particle interactions, such as electron-positron annihilation, neutral pion decay, radioactive decay, fusion, fission or inverse Compton scattering in astrophysical processes. _____ typically have frequencies above 10^{19} Hz and therefore energies above 100 keV and wavelength less than 10 picometers, often smaller than an atom.
   a. 1509 Istanbul earthquake
   b. 1703 Genroku earthquake
   c. 1700 Cascadia earthquake
   d. Gamma rays

28. The _____ of a quantity whose value decreases with time is the interval required for the quantity to decay to half of its initial value. The concept originated in describing how long it takes atoms to undergo radioactive decay but also applies in a wide variety of other situations.
   a. 1703 Genroku earthquake
   b. 1700 Cascadia earthquake
   c. 1509 Istanbul earthquake
   d. Half-life

29. In physics, _____ describes any process in which energy emitted by one body travels through a medium or through space, ultimately to be absorbed by another body. Non-physicists often associate the word with ionizing _____, but it can also refer to electromagnetic _____ (i.e., radio waves, infrared light, visible light, ultraviolet light, and X-rays) which can also be ionizing _____, to acoustic _____, or to other more obscure processes. What makes it _____ is that the energy radiates (i.e., it travels outward in straight lines in all directions) from the source.
   a. Radiation
   b. 1703 Genroku earthquake
   c. 1509 Istanbul earthquake
   d. 1700 Cascadia earthquake

30. The _____ Era, is the most recent of the three classic geological eras and covers the period from 65.5 million years ago to the present. It is marked by the Cretaceous-Tertiary extinction event at the end of the Cretaceous that saw the demise of the last non-avian dinosaurs and the end of the Mesozoic Era. The _____ era is ongoing.
   a. 1509 Istanbul earthquake
   b. 1700 Cascadia earthquake
   c. 1703 Genroku earthquake
   d. Cenozoic

31. In stratigraphy, _____ is the native consolidated rock underlying the surface of a terrestrial planet, usually the Earth. Above the _____ is usually an area of broken and weathered unconsolidated rock in the basal subsoil. The top of the _____ is known as rockhead and identifying this, via excavations, drilling or geophysical methods, is an important task in most civil engineering projects.

a. Sequence stratigraphy
c. Polystrate
b. Biozones
d. Bedrock

32. _____ are the largest glaciers, enormous masses of ice that are not visibly affected by the landscape and that cover the entire surface beneath them, except possibly on the margins where they are thinnest. Antarctica and Greenland are the only places where continental _____ currently exist. These regions contain vast quantities of fresh water.
   a. AL 333
   b. AASHTO Soil Classification System
   c. Ice sheets
   d. AL 129-1

33. The _____ was proposed by the Danish geological pioneer Nicholas Steno (1638-1686.) This principle states that layers of sediment are originally deposited horizontally. The principle is important to the analysis of folded and tilted strata.
   a. Bedrock
   b. Cyclostratigraphy
   c. Key bed
   d. Principle of Original Horizontality

34. _____ is a common and widely occurring type of intrusive, felsic, igneous rock. _____ has a medium to coarse texture, occasionally with some individual crystals larger than the groundmass forming a rock known as porphyry. _____s can be pink to dark gray or even black, depending on their chemistry and mineralogy.
   a. 1700 Cascadia earthquake
   b. 1703 Genroku earthquake
   c. 1509 Istanbul earthquake
   d. Granite

35. _____ is a type of rock consisting of consolidated volcanic ash ejected from vents during a volcanic eruption. _____ is sometimes called tufa, particularly when used as construction material, although tufa also refers to a quite different rock.

The products of a volcanic eruption are volcanic gases, lava, steam, and tephra. Magma is blown apart when it interacts violently with volcanic gases and steam. Solid material produced and thrown into the air by such volcanic eruptions is called tephra, regardless of composition or fragment size. If the resulting pieces of ejecta are small enough, the material is called volcanic ash, defined as such particles less than 2 mm in diameter, sand-sized or smaller.

   a. Tuff
   b. Coldwell Complex
   c. Welded tuff
   d. Charnockite

36. _____ is a process of converting a material into a glass-like amorphous solid that is free from any crystalline structure, either by the quick removal or addition of heat, or by mixing with an additive. Solidification of a vitreous solid occurs at the glass transition temperature (which is lower than melting temperature, T_m, due to supercooling.)

When the starting material is solid, _____ usually involves heating the substances to very high temperatures.

   a. 1703 Genroku earthquake
   b. 1700 Cascadia earthquake
   c. 1509 Istanbul earthquake
   d. Vitrification

37. _____ is a pyroclastic rock, of any origin, that was sufficiently hot at the time of deposition to weld together. Strictly speaking, if the rock contains scattered pea-sized fragments or fiamme in it, it is called a welded lapilli-tuff. They (and welded lapilli-tuffs) can be of fallout origin, or deposited from pyroclastic density currents, as in the case of ignimbrites.

a. Country rock
c. Charnockite
b. Coldwell Complex
d. Welded tuff

Chapter 16. Water Pollution

1. _____ is a broadly useful concept that expresses how fast something moves through a system in equilibrium. It is the average time a substance spends within a specified region of space, such as a reservoir. For example, the _____ of water stored in deep groundwater, as part of the water cycle, is about 10,000 years.
   a. 1700 Cascadia earthquake
   b. 1703 Genroku earthquake
   c. Residence time
   d. 1509 Istanbul earthquake

2. _____ is a carbonate mineral and the most stable polymorph of calcium carbonate ($CaCO_3$.) The other polymorphs are the minerals aragonite and vaterite. Aragonite will change to _____ at 470>°C, and vaterite is even less stable.

   _____ is a common constituent of sedimentary rocks, limestone in particular, much of which is formed from the shells of dead marine organisms. Approximately 10% of sedimentary rock is limestone.

   a. 1700 Cascadia earthquake
   b. Calcite
   c. 1509 Istanbul earthquake
   d. 1703 Genroku earthquake

3. _____ is the water flow which occurs when soil is infiltrated to full capacity and excess water, from rain, snowmelt, or other sources flows over the land. This is a major component of the hydrologic cycle. Runoff that occurs on surfaces before reaching a channel is also called a nonpoint source.
   a. 1700 Cascadia earthquake
   b. Surface runoff
   c. Thermal pollution
   d. 1509 Istanbul earthquake

4. The _____ provides a uniform system of measuring pollution levels for the major air pollutants. It is based on a scale devised by the United States Environmental Protection Agency (USEPA) to provide a way for broadcasts and newspapers to report air quality on a daily basis.

   The _____ is reported as a number on a scale of 0 to 500 and is the air quality indicator.

   a. 1700 Cascadia earthquake
   b. Pollutant Standards Index
   c. 1509 Istanbul earthquake
   d. 1703 Genroku earthquake

5. The _____ is the epoch from 1.8 million to 11550 years BP covering the world's recent period of repeated glaciations. The _____ epoch follows the Pliocene epoch and is followed by the Holocene epoch. The _____ is the third epoch of the Neogene period or 6th epoch of the Cenozoic Era. The end of the _____ corresponds with the retreat of the last continental glacier. It also corresponds with the end of the Paleolithic age used in archaeology.
   a. Late Pleistocene
   b. Tyrrhenian
   c. Pleistocene
   d. Sicilian Stage

6. _____, also known as the Pleistocene glaciation, the current ice age or simply the ice age, refers to the period of the last few million years in which permanent ice sheets were established in Antarctica and perhaps Greenland, and fluctuating ice sheets have occurred elsewhere The major effects of the ice age were erosion and deposition of material over large parts of the continents, modification of river systems, creation of millions of lakes, changes in sea level, development of pluvial lakes far from the ice margins, isostatic adjustment of the crust, and abnormal winds. It affected oceans, flooding, and biological communities.
   a. Glacial period
   b. Quaternary glaciation
   c. Bergschrund
   d. Wolstonian Stage

Chapter 16. Water Pollution

7. The _____ Era is one of three geologic eras of the Phanerozoic eon. The division of time into eras dates back to Giovanni Arduino, in the 18th century, although his original name for the era now called the '_____' was 'Secondary' (making the modern era the 'Tertiary'.)

The _____ was a time of tectonic, climatic and evolutionary activity. The continents gradually shifted from a state of connectedness into their present configuration; the drifting provided for speciation and other important evolutionary developments.

   a. 1703 Genroku earthquake
   b. Mesozoic
   c. 1509 Istanbul earthquake
   d. 1700 Cascadia earthquake

8. The _____ characterizes the scratch resistance of various minerals through the ability of a harder material to scratch a softer material. It was created in 1812 by the German mineralogist Friedrich Mohs and is one of several definitions of hardness in materials science. The method, however, is of great antiquity, having first been mentioned by Theophrastus in his treatise On Stones in ca 300 BC, followed by Pliny the Elder in his Naturalis Historia circa A.D.
   a. 1703 Genroku earthquake
   b. 1700 Cascadia earthquake
   c. Mohs scale of mineral hardness
   d. 1509 Istanbul earthquake

9. Traditionally, _____ compounds are considered to be of a mineral, not biological, origin. Complementarily, most organic compounds are traditionally viewed as being of biological origin. Over the past century, the precise classification of _____ vs organic compounds has become less important to scientists, primarily because the majority of known compounds are synthetic and not of natural origin.

Minerals are mainly oxides and sulfides, which are strictly _____. In fact, most of the earth and the universe is _____. Although the components of the Earth's crust are well elucidated, the processes of mineralization and the composition of the deep mantle remain active areas of investigation, which are mainly covered in geology-oriented venues.

   a. AASHTO Soil Classification System
   b. AL 129-1
   c. AL 333
   d. Inorganic

10. A _____ is an opening in a planet's surface or crust, which allows hot, molten rock, ash, and gases to escape from below the surface. Volcanic activity involving the extrusion of rock tends to form mountains or features like mountains over a period of time.
   a. 1700 Cascadia earthquake
   b. Volcano
   c. 1703 Genroku earthquake
   d. 1509 Istanbul earthquake

11. The _____ is a geologic fault zone capable of generating significantly destructive earthquakes. About 60 kilometers long, it lies mainly along the western base of the hills on the east side of San Francisco Bay. It runs through densely-populated areas, including the cities of Richmond, El Cerrito, Berkeley, Oakland, San Leandro, Hayward, Fremont, and San Jose.

The _____ is parallel to its more famous (and much longer) westerly neighbor, the San Andreas Fault, which lies offshore and through the San Francisco peninsula.

a. 1700 Cascadia earthquake
c. Hayward Fault Zone

b. 1703 Genroku earthquake
d. 1509 Istanbul earthquake

12. A _____ or sandbar is a somewhat linear landform within or extending into a body of water, typically composed of sand, silt or small pebbles. A bar is characteristically long and narrow and develops where a stream or ocean current promotes deposition of granular material, resulting in localized shallowing of the water. Bars can appear in the sea, in a lake, or in a river.

The term _____ can be applied to larger geological units that form off a coastline as part of the process of coastal erosion. These include spits and baymouth bars that form across the front of embayments and rias. A tombolo is a bar that forms an isthmus between an island or offshore rock and a mainland shore.

a. Shoal
c. 1703 Genroku earthquake

b. 1700 Cascadia earthquake
d. 1509 Istanbul earthquake

13. In geology, a _____ or _____ line is a planar fracture in rock in which the rock on one side of the fracture has moved with respect to the rock on the other side. Large _____s within the Earth's crust are the result of differential or shear motion and active _____ zones are the causal locations of most earthquakes. Earthquakes are caused by energy release during rapid slippage along a _____.

a. Fault
c. Stack

b. Streak
d. Tarn

14. A _____ is a member of an ill-defined subset of elements that exhibit metallic properties, which would mainly include the transition metals, some metalloids, lanthanides, and actinides. Many different definitions have been proposed--some based on density, some on atomic number or atomic weight, and some on chemical properties or toxicity. The term _____ has been called 'meaningless and misleading' in an IUPAC technical report due to the contradictory definitions and its lack of a 'coherent scientific basis'.

a. Cohesion
c. Drainage system

b. Heavy metal
d. Submersion

15. A _____ is a mountain rising from the ocean seafloor that does not reach to the water's surface (sea level), and thus is not an island. These are typically formed from extinct volcanoes, that rise abruptly and are usually found rising from a seafloor of 1,000-4,000 meters depth. They are defined by oceanographers as independent features that rise to at least 1,000 meters above the seafloor.

a. Seamount
c. 1703 Genroku earthquake

b. 1700 Cascadia earthquake
d. 1509 Istanbul earthquake

16. An _____ is an underground layer of water-bearing permeable rock or unconsolidated materials (gravel, sand, silt, or clay) from which groundwater can be usefully extracted using a water well. The study of water flow in _____s and the characterization of _____s is called hydrogeology. Related terms include: an aquitard, which is an impermeable layer along an _____, and an aquiclude (or aquifuge), which is a solid, impermeable area beneath an _____.

a. Aquifer
c. AL 129-1

b. AL 333
d. AASHTO Soil Classification System

Chapter 16. Water Pollution

17. _____ is water located beneath the ground surface in soil pore spaces and in the fractures of lithologic formations. A unit of rock or an unconsolidated deposit is called an aquifer when it can yield a usable quantity of water. The depth at which soil pore spaces or fractures and voids in rock become completely saturated with water is called the water table.
   a. 1700 Cascadia earthquake
   b. Groundwater
   c. Depression focused recharge
   d. 1509 Istanbul earthquake

18. _____ is an organometallic cation with the formula $[CH_3Hg]^+$. It is a bioaccumulative environmental toxicant.

   '_____' is a shorthand for 'monomethylmercury', and is more correctly 'monomethylmercuric cation'.

   a. 1703 Genroku earthquake
   b. 1700 Cascadia earthquake
   c. 1509 Istanbul earthquake
   d. Methylmercury

19. Organic chemistry is the science concerned with all aspects of _____. Organic synthesis is the methodology of their preparation.

   The name 'organic' is historical, dating back to the 19th century, when it was believed that _____ could only be synthesized in living organisms through vis vitalis - the 'life-force'.

   a. AASHTO Soil Classification System
   b. Organic compounds
   c. AL 333
   d. AL 129-1

20. _____ is the naturally occurring, unconsolidated or loose covering on the Earth's surface. _____ is composed of particles of broken rock that have been altered by chemical, biological and environmental processes including weathering and erosion. _____ is different from its parent rock(s) source(s), altered by interactions between the lithosphere, hydrosphere, atmosphere, and the biosphere.
   a. Slump
   b. Soil
   c. 1509 Istanbul earthquake
   d. Topsoil

21. The _____ is a vast yet shallow underground water table aquifer located beneath the Great Plains in the United States. One of the world's largest aquifers, it covers an area of approximately 174,000 mi^2 in portions of the eight states of South Dakota, Nebraska, Wyoming, Colorado, Kansas, Oklahoma, New Mexico, and Texas. It was named in 1898 by N.H. Darton from its type locality near the town of Ogallala, Nebraska.
   a. Ogallala aquifer
   b. AL 129-1
   c. AASHTO Soil Classification System
   d. AL 333

22. A _____ column (or _____) is a column of rising air in the lower altitudes of the Earth's atmosphere. They are created by the uneven heating of the Earth's surface from solar radiation, and an example of convection. The Sun warms the ground, which in turn warms the air directly above it.
   a. Thermal
   b. 1700 Cascadia earthquake
   c. 1509 Istanbul earthquake
   d. 1703 Genroku earthquake

Chapter 16. Water Pollution

23. _____ is the degradation of water quality by any process that changes ambient water temperature. A common cause of _____ is the use of water as a coolant by power plants and industrial manufacturers. When water used as a coolant is returned to the natural environment at a higher temperature, the change in temperature impacts organisms by (a) decreasing oxygen supply, and (b) affecting ecosystem composition.
   a. Surface runoff
   b. Thermal pollution
   c. 1509 Istanbul earthquake
   d. 1700 Cascadia earthquake

24. _____ is a large 13 kilometres wide caldera situated to the west of Naples, Italy declared regional park in 2003. Today mostly lying underwater, the area comprises 24 craters and volcanic edifices, some of which present hydrothermal activity at Lucrino, Agnano and the town of Pozzuoli and effusive gaseous manifestations like the Solfatara crater, mythological home of the Roman god of fire, Vulcan. The area also features bradyseismic phenomena, which are most evident at the temple of Serapis in Pozzuoli.
   a. 1509 Istanbul earthquake
   b. 1700 Cascadia earthquake
   c. 1703 Genroku earthquake
   d. Campi Flegrei

25. _____ or Biological Oxygen Demand is a chemical procedure for determining how fast biological organisms use up oxygen in a body of water. It is used in water quality management and assessment, ecology and environmental science.
   _____ is not an accurate quantitative test, although it could be considered as an indication of the quality of a water source.
   a. 1509 Istanbul earthquake
   b. 1700 Cascadia earthquake
   c. Biogas
   d. Biochemical oxygen demand

26. A _____, sometimes called a composite volcano, is a tall, conical volcano with many layers (strata) of hardened lava, tephra, and volcanic ash. They are characterized by a steep profile and periodic, explosive eruptions. The lava that flows from a _____ tends to be viscous; it cools and hardens before spreading far.
   a. Mount Overlord
   b. Mount Baker
   c. Stratovolcano
   d. Nevado Sajama

27. _____ is an increase in chemical nutrients -- compounds containing nitrogen or phosphorus -- in an ecosystem, and may occur on land or in water. However, the term is often used to mean the resultant increase in the ecosystem's primary productivity (excessive plant growth and decay), and further effects including lack of oxygen and severe reductions in water quality, fish, and other animal populations. Though this image has a noticeable cyan tint, the _____ of the Potomac River is evident from its bright green water, caused by a dense bloom of cyanobacteria.

   _____ is frequently a result of nutrient pollution, such as the release of sewage effluent, urban stormwater run-off, and run-off carrying excess fertilizers into natural waters.

   a. Eutrophication
   b. Overland flow
   c. AASHTO Soil Classification System
   d. Intertidal

28. _____ is the movement of the Earth's continents relative to each other. The hypothesis that continents 'drift' was first put forward by Abraham Ortelius in 1596 and was fully developed by Alfred Wegener in 1912. However, it was not until the development of the theory of plate tectonics in the 1960s, that a sufficient geological explanation of that movement was found.
   a. Subduction
   b. Continental drift
   c. Thrust fault
   d. Plate tectonics

Chapter 16. Water Pollution

29. In geology, _____ is transported rock debris overlying the solid bedrock. The term is also sometimes refers to organic debris so-transported. In the largest sense, it refers to the material left behind by retreating continental glaciers.
   a. Duricrust
   b. Gibraltar Arc
   c. Fulgurites
   d. Drift

30. _____ is molten rock that is found beneath the surface of the Earth, and may also exist on other terrestrial planets. Besides molten rock, _____ may also contain suspended crystals and gas bubbles. _____ often collects in a _____ chamber inside a volcano. _____ is capable of intrusion into adjacent rocks, extrusion onto the surface as lava, and explosive ejection as tephra to form pyroclastic rock.
   a. Pluton
   b. Laccolith
   c. Volcanic rock
   d. Magma

31. _____ is organic matter used as organic fertilizer in agriculture. _____s contribute to the fertility of the soil by adding organic matter and nutrients, such as nitrogen that is trapped by bacteria in the soil. Higher organisms then feed on the fungi and bacteria in a chain of life that comprises the soil food web.
   a. 1509 Istanbul earthquake
   b. Manure
   c. 1700 Cascadia earthquake
   d. 1703 Genroku earthquake

32. _____ is any particulate matter that can be transported by fluid flow, and which eventually is deposited.

They are most often transported by water (fluvial processes) transported by wind (aeolian processes) and glaciers. Beach sands and river channel deposits are examples of fluvial transport and deposition, though _____ also often settles out of slow-moving or standing water in lakes and oceans.

   a. Fech fech
   b. Brickearth
   c. Dry quicksand
   d. Sediment

33. _____ is an excavation activity or operation usually carried out at least partly underwater, in shallow seas or fresh water areas with the purpose of gathering up bottom sediments and disposing of them at a different location.

This technique is often used to keep waterways navigable. It is also used as a way to replenish sand on some public beaches, where too much sand has been lost because of coastal erosion.

   a. Dredging
   b. 1509 Istanbul earthquake
   c. 1703 Genroku earthquake
   d. 1700 Cascadia earthquake

34. _____ is water collecting on the ground or in a stream, river, lake, wetland, or ocean; it is related to water collecting as groundwater or atmospheric water.

_____ is naturally replenished by precipitation and naturally lost through discharge to evaporation, and sub-surface seepage into the groundwater. Although there are other sources of groundwater, such as connate water and magmatic water, precipitation is the major one and groundwater originated in this way is called meteoric water.

Chapter 16. Water Pollution

a. Surface water
c. Cone of depression
b. Vadose zone
d. Flood stage

35. _____ is the process of cleansing to remove contamination, or the possibility (or fear) of contamination. _____ is sometimes abbreviated as 'decon', 'dcon', or 'decontam'.

Persons suspected of being contaminated are usually separated by sex, and led into a decon tent, a decon trailer, or a decon pod, where they shed their potentially contamined clothes in a stripdown room.

a. 1509 Istanbul earthquake
c. 1703 Genroku earthquake
b. 1700 Cascadia earthquake
d. Decontamination

36. _____ can be defined as any process that uses microorganisms, fungi, green plants or their enzymes to return the natural environment altered by contaminants to its original condition. _____ may be employed to attack specific soil contaminants, such as degradation of chlorinated hydrocarbons by bacteria. An example of a more general approach is the cleanup of oil spills by the addition of nitrate and/or sulfate fertilisers to facilitate the decomposition of crude oil by indigenous or exogenous bacteria.

a. 1703 Genroku earthquake
c. 1700 Cascadia earthquake
b. 1509 Istanbul earthquake
d. Bioremediation

37. _____ is the transferring of volatile components of a liquid into an air stream. It is a chemical engineering technology used for the purification of groundwaters and wastewaters containing volatile compounds.

Volatile compounds have relatively high vapor pressure and low aqueous solubility characterized by the compound'e;s dimensionless Henry's law coefficient, which is the ratio of the concentration in air that is in equilibrium with its concentration in water.

a. AL 129-1
c. AL 333
b. Air stripping
d. AASHTO Soil Classification System

Chapter 17. Air Pollution

1. _____ is a branch of atmospheric science in which the chemistry of the Earth's atmosphere and that of other planets is studied. It is a multidisciplinary field of research and draws on environmental chemistry, physics, meteorology, computer modeling, oceanography, geology and volcanology and other disciplines. Research is increasingly connected with other areas of study such as climatology.
    a. AASHTO Soil Classification System
    b. Atmospheric chemistry
    c. Atmospheric oxygenation event
    d. AL 129-1

2. _____ is a broadly useful concept that expresses how fast something moves through a system in equilibrium. It is the average time a substance spends within a specified region of space, such as a reservoir. For example, the _____ of water stored in deep groundwater, as part of the water cycle, is about 10,000 years.
    a. 1509 Istanbul earthquake
    b. 1700 Cascadia earthquake
    c. Residence time
    d. 1703 Genroku earthquake

3. Volatile organic compounds (_____) are gases or vapours emitted by various solids or liquids, many of which have short- and long-term adverse health effects. Household products that emit _____ include paint, paint strippers, cleaning supplies, pesticides, glues and adhesives, building materials and furnishings. Consequently, concentrations of many _____ are higher indoors (up to ten times higher) than outdoors.
    a. VOCs
    b. 1703 Genroku earthquake
    c. 1509 Istanbul earthquake
    d. 1700 Cascadia earthquake

4. Organic chemistry is the science concerned with all aspects of _____. Organic synthesis is the methodology of their preparation.

The name 'organic' is historical, dating back to the 19th century, when it was believed that _____ could only be synthesized in living organisms through vis vitalis - the 'life-force'.

    a. AL 333
    b. AL 129-1
    c. AASHTO Soil Classification System
    d. Organic compounds

5. _____s, alternatively referred to as _____ matter (PM) or fine particles, are tiny particles of solid or liquid suspended in a gas or liquid. In contrast, aerosol refers to particles and the gas together. Sources of _____ matter can be man made or natural.
    a. Particulate
    b. 1703 Genroku earthquake
    c. 1509 Istanbul earthquake
    d. 1700 Cascadia earthquake

6. _____ are gases or vapours emitted by various solids or liquids, many of which have short- and long-term adverse health effects. Household products that emit _____s include paint, paint strippers, cleaning supplies, pesticides, glues and adhesives, building materials and furnishings. Consequently, concentrations of many _____s are higher indoors (up to ten times higher) than outdoors.
    a. 1703 Genroku earthquake
    b. 1700 Cascadia earthquake
    c. 1509 Istanbul earthquake
    d. Volatile organic compounds

7. _____ is a large 13 kilometres wide caldera situated to the west of Naples, Italy declared regional park in 2003. Today mostly lying underwater, the area comprises 24 craters and volcanic edifices, some of which present hydrothermal activity at Lucrino, Agnano and the town of Pozzuoli and effusive gaseous manifestations like the Solfatara crater, mythological home of the Roman god of fire, Vulcan. The area also features bradyseismic phenomena, which are most evident at the temple of Serapis in Pozzuoli.

Chapter 17. Air Pollution

    a. 1700 Cascadia earthquake
    b. 1509 Istanbul earthquake
    c. 1703 Genroku earthquake
    d. Campi Flegrei

8. In physics, _____ describes any process in which energy emitted by one body travels through a medium or through space, ultimately to be absorbed by another body. Non-physicists often associate the word with ionizing _____, but it can also refer to electromagnetic _____ (i.e., radio waves, infrared light, visible light, ultraviolet light, and X-rays) which can also be ionizing _____, to acoustic _____, or to other more obscure processes. What makes it _____ is that the energy radiates (i.e., it travels outward in straight lines in all directions) from the source.

    a. 1509 Istanbul earthquake
    b. Radiation
    c. 1703 Genroku earthquake
    d. 1700 Cascadia earthquake

9. _____ is soil or rock derived granular material of a grain size between sand and clay. _____ may occur as a soil or as suspended sediment in a surface water body. It may also exist as soil deposited at the bottom of a water body.

    a. 1700 Cascadia earthquake
    b. 1509 Istanbul earthquake
    c. 1703 Genroku earthquake
    d. Silt

10. _____ is a form of extractive metallurgy; its main use is to produce a metal from its ore. This includes iron extraction (for the production of steel) from iron ore, and copper extraction and other base metals from their ores. _____ uses heat and a chemical reducing agent, commonly a fuel that is a source of carbon such as coke, or in earlier times charcoal, to change the oxidation state of the metal ore.

    a. 1700 Cascadia earthquake
    b. Smelting
    c. 1703 Genroku earthquake
    d. 1509 Istanbul earthquake

11. The _____ Era is one of three geologic eras of the Phanerozoic eon. The division of time into eras dates back to Giovanni Arduino, in the 18th century, although his original name for the era now called the '_____' was 'Secondary' (making the modern era the 'Tertiary'.)

The _____ was a time of tectonic, climatic and evolutionary activity. The continents gradually shifted from a state of connectedness into their present configuration; the drifting provided for speciation and other important evolutionary developments.

    a. 1703 Genroku earthquake
    b. 1509 Istanbul earthquake
    c. Mesozoic
    d. 1700 Cascadia earthquake

12. A _____ or sandbar is a somewhat linear landform within or extending into a body of water, typically composed of sand, silt or small pebbles. A bar is characteristically long and narrow and develops where a stream or ocean current promotes deposition of granular material, resulting in localized shallowing of the water. Bars can appear in the sea, in a lake, or in a river.

The term _____ can be applied to larger geological units that form off a coastline as part of the process of coastal erosion. These include spits and baymouth bars that form across the front of embayments and rias. A tombolo is a bar that forms an isthmus between an island or offshore rock and a mainland shore.

    a. 1509 Istanbul earthquake
    b. Shoal
    c. 1700 Cascadia earthquake
    d. 1703 Genroku earthquake

Chapter 17. Air Pollution

13. A _____ is a mountain rising from the ocean seafloor that does not reach to the water's surface (sea level), and thus is not an island. These are typically formed from extinct volcanoes, that rise abruptly and are usually found rising from a seafloor of 1,000-4,000 meters depth. They are defined by oceanographers as independent features that rise to at least 1,000 meters above the seafloor.
    a. 1700 Cascadia earthquake
    b. 1703 Genroku earthquake
    c. 1509 Istanbul earthquake
    d. Seamount

14. _____ is a chemical element with symbol Rn and atomic number 86. _____ is a colorless, odorless, tasteless, naturally occurring, radioactive noble gas that is formed from the decay of radium. It is one of the heaviest substances that remains a gas under normal conditions and is considered to be a health hazard.
    a. 1703 Genroku earthquake
    b. Radon
    c. 1509 Istanbul earthquake
    d. 1700 Cascadia earthquake

15. A _____ column (or _____) is a column of rising air in the lower altitudes of the Earth's atmosphere. They are created by the uneven heating of the Earth's surface from solar radiation, and an example of convection. The Sun warms the ground, which in turn warms the air directly above it.
    a. 1509 Istanbul earthquake
    b. 1700 Cascadia earthquake
    c. 1703 Genroku earthquake
    d. Thermal

16. The _____ is an informal name for the supereon comprising the eons of the geologic timescale that came before the current Phanerozoic eon. It spans from the formation of Earth around 4500 Mya (million years ago) to the evolution of abundant macroscopic hard-shelled animals, which marked the beginning of the Cambrian, the first period of the first era of the Phanerozoic eon, some 542 Mya. It is named after the Roman name for Wales - Cambria - where rocks from this age were first studied.
    a. 1509 Istanbul earthquake
    b. 1700 Cascadia earthquake
    c. 1703 Genroku earthquake
    d. Precambrian

17. The _____ provides a uniform system of measuring pollution levels for the major air pollutants. It is based on a scale devised by the United States Environmental Protection Agency (USEPA) to provide a way for broadcasts and newspapers to report air quality on a daily basis.

    The _____ is reported as a number on a scale of 0 to 500 and is the air quality indicator.

    a. Pollutant Standards Index
    b. 1703 Genroku earthquake
    c. 1509 Istanbul earthquake
    d. 1700 Cascadia earthquake

18. A _____ is an opening in a planet's surface or crust, which allows hot, molten rock, ash, and gases to escape from below the surface. Volcanic activity involving the extrusion of rock tends to form mountains or features like mountains over a period of time.
    a. 1703 Genroku earthquake
    b. 1700 Cascadia earthquake
    c. Volcano
    d. 1509 Istanbul earthquake

Chapter 17. Air Pollution

19. An _____, or electrostatic air cleaner is a particulate collection device that removes particles from a flowing gas (such as air) using the force of an induced electrostatic charge. _____s are highly efficient filtration devices that minimally impede the flow of gases through the device, and can easily remove fine particulate matter such as dust and smoke from the air stream. In contrast to wet scrubbers which apply energy directly to the flowing fluid medium, an ESP applies energy only to the particulate matter being collected and therefore is very efficient in its consumption of energy (in the form of electricity.)

   a. AASHTO Soil Classification System
   b. AL 129-1
   c. AL 333
   d. Electrostatic precipitator

20. A _____ describes one of a number of pieces of legislation relating to the reduction of smog and air pollution in general. The use by governments to enforce clean air standards has contributed to an improvement in human health and longer life spans. Critics argue it has also sapped corporate profits and contributed to outsourcing, while defenders counter that improved environmental air quality has generated more jobs than it has eliminated.

   a. 1700 Cascadia earthquake
   b. 1703 Genroku earthquake
   c. Clean Air Act
   d. 1509 Istanbul earthquake

21. In inorganic chemistry, a _____ is a salt of sulfuric acid.

The _____ ion is a polyatomic anion with the empirical formula SO_4^{2-} and a molecular mass of 96.06 daltons; it consists of a central sulfur atom surrounded by four equivalent oxygen atoms in a tetrahedral arrangement. The sulfur atom is in the +6 oxidation state while the four oxygen atoms are each in the -2 state.

   a. 1703 Genroku earthquake
   b. 1509 Istanbul earthquake
   c. 1700 Cascadia earthquake
   d. Sulfate

Chapter 18. Environmental Law

1. The _____ is an area where large numbers of earthquakes and volcanic eruptions occur in the basin of the Pacific Ocean. In a 40,000 km horseshoe shape, it is associated with a nearly continuous series of oceanic trenches, volcanic arcs, and volcanic belts and/or plate movements. The _____ has 452 volcanoes and is home to over 75% of the world's active and dormant volcanoes.
    a. 1700 Cascadia earthquake
    b. 1703 Genroku earthquake
    c. 1509 Istanbul earthquake
    d. Pacific Ring of Fire

2. A _____ zone or _____ area is the interface between land and a stream. Plant communities along the river margins are called _____ vegetation, characterized by hydrophilic plants. _____ zones are significant in ecology, environmental management, and civil engineering because of their role in soil conservation, their biodiversity, and the influence they have on aquatic ecosystems.
    a. 1509 Istanbul earthquake
    b. Riparian
    c. 1703 Genroku earthquake
    d. 1700 Cascadia earthquake

3. The _____ is the world's third deep geological repository licensed to permanently dispose of transuranic radioactive waste for 10000 years that is left from the research and production of nuclear weapons and nuclear power plants. It is located approximately 26 miles east of Carlsbad, New Mexico, in eastern Eddy County.
    a. 1703 Genroku earthquake
    b. Waste Isolation Pilot Plant
    c. 1509 Istanbul earthquake
    d. 1700 Cascadia earthquake

4. _____ is water collecting on the ground or in a stream, river, lake, wetland, or ocean; it is related to water collecting as groundwater or atmospheric water.

   _____ is naturally replenished by precipitation and naturally lost through discharge to evaporation, and sub-surface seepage into the groundwater. Although there are other sources of groundwater, such as connate water and magmatic water, precipitation is the major one and groundwater originated in this way is called meteoric water.

    a. Flood stage
    b. Vadose zone
    c. Cone of depression
    d. Surface water

5. Under the law of the sea, an _____ is a seazone over which a state has special rights over the exploration and use of marine resources. It stretches from the edge of the state's territorial sea out to 200 nautical miles from its coast. In casual use, the term may include the territorial sea and even the continental shelf beyond the 200 mile limit.
    a. AL 129-1
    b. AASHTO Soil Classification System
    c. AL 333
    d. Exclusive Economic Zone

6. The _____ or law of capture is common law from England, adopted by a number of U.S. jurisdictions, that determines ownership of captured natural resources including groundwater, oil, gas, and game animals. The general rule is that the first person to 'capture' such a resource owns that resource. For example, a landowner who extracts or 'e;captures'e; groundwater, oil, or gas from a well that bottoms within the subsurface of his land acquires absolute ownership of the substance, even if it is drained from the subsurface of another'e;s land.
    a. Surface Mining Control and Reclamation Act
    b. Rule of Capture
    c. Toxic Substances Control Act
    d. General Mining Act of 1872

Chapter 18. Environmental Law

7. The _____ doctrine is a legal doctrine limiting the rights of landowners to a common source of groundwater (such as an aquifer) to a reasonable share, typically based on the amount of land owned by each on the surface above. This doctrine is also applied to oil and gas in some U.S. states.

Under California law, the owners of overlying land own the subsurface water as tenants in common, and each is allowed a reasonable amount for his/her own use.

- a. Correlative rights
- b. 1509 Istanbul earthquake
- c. 1703 Genroku earthquake
- d. 1700 Cascadia earthquake

8. _____ is water located beneath the ground surface in soil pore spaces and in the fractures of lithologic formations. A unit of rock or an unconsolidated deposit is called an aquifer when it can yield a usable quantity of water. The depth at which soil pore spaces or fractures and voids in rock become completely saturated with water is called the water table.
- a. Depression focused recharge
- b. Groundwater
- c. 1509 Istanbul earthquake
- d. 1700 Cascadia earthquake

9. The _____ is the extended perimeter of each continent and associated coastal plain, and was part of the continent during the glacial periods, but is undersea during interglacial periods such as the current epoch by relatively shallow seas (known as shelf seas) and gulfs.

The continental rise is below the slope, but landward of the abyssal plains. Its gradient is intermediate between the slope and the shelf, on the order of 0.5-1°.

- a. 1509 Istanbul earthquake
- b. Surface runoff
- c. 1700 Cascadia earthquake
- d. Continental Shelf

10. The _____ characterizes the scratch resistance of various minerals through the ability of a harder material to scratch a softer material. It was created in 1812 by the German mineralogist Friedrich Mohs and is one of several definitions of hardness in materials science. The method, however, is of great antiquity, having first been mentioned by Theophrastus in his treatise On Stones in ca 300 BC, followed by Pliny the Elder in his Naturalis Historia circa A.D.
- a. 1700 Cascadia earthquake
- b. 1703 Genroku earthquake
- c. 1509 Istanbul earthquake
- d. Mohs scale of mineral hardness

11. _____ is a type of mining in which soil and rock overlying the mineral deposit are removed. It is the opposite of underground mining, in which the overlying rock is left in place, and the mineral removed through shafts or tunnels.

_____ is used when deposits of commercially useful minerals or rock are found near the surface; that is, where the overburden (surface material covering the valuable deposit) is relatively thin or the material of interest is structurally unsuitable for tunneling (as would usually be the case for sand, cinder, and gravel.)

- a. 1703 Genroku earthquake
- b. 1700 Cascadia earthquake
- c. 1509 Istanbul earthquake
- d. Surface Mining

12. The _____ of 1977 (SMCRA) is the primary federal law that regulates the environmental effects of coal mining in the United States.

SMCRA created two programs: one for regulating active coal mines and a second for reclaiming abandoned mine lands. SMCRA also created the Office of Surface Mining, an agency within the Department of the Interior, to promulgate regulations, to fund state regulatory and reclamation efforts, and to ensure consistency among state regulatory programs.

a. General Mining Act of 1872
b. Surface Mining Control and Reclamation Act
c. Rule of Capture
d. Toxic Substances Control Act

13. _____ is the process of creating useful landscapes that meet a variety of goals, typically creating productive ecosystems (or sometimes industrial or municipal land) from mined land. It includes all aspects of this work, including material placement, stabilizing, capping, regrading, placing cover soils, revegetation, and maintenance.

In the USA, _____ is a regular part of modern mining practice.

a. 1700 Cascadia earthquake
b. 1509 Istanbul earthquake
c. 1703 Genroku earthquake
d. Mine reclamation

14. A _____ or sea vent, is a type of hydrothermal vent found on the ocean floor. They are formed in fields hundreds of meters wide when superheated water from below Earth's crust comes through the ocean floor. This water is rich in dissolved minerals from the crust, most notably sulfides.

a. 1703 Genroku earthquake
b. Black smoker
c. 1509 Istanbul earthquake
d. 1700 Cascadia earthquake

15. _____ circulation in its most general sense is the circulation of hot water; 'hydros' in the Greek meaning water and 'thermos' meaning heat. _____ circulation occurs most often in the vicinity of sources of heat within the Earth's crust. This generally occurs near volcanic activity, but can occur in the deep crust related to the intrusion of granite, or as the result of orogeny or metamorphism.

a. Seafloor spreading
b. Permineralization
c. Hydrothermal
d. Stoping

16. A _____ is a fissure in a planet's surface from which geothermally heated water issues. they are commonly found near volcanically active places, areas where tectonic plates are moving apart, ocean basins, and hotspots.

They are locally very common because the earth is both geologically active and has large amounts of water on its surface and within its crust. Common land types include hot springs, fumaroles and geysers. The most famous _____ system on land is probably within Yellowstone National Park in the United States.

a. Hydrothermal vent
b. 1700 Cascadia earthquake
c. 1703 Genroku earthquake
d. 1509 Istanbul earthquake

17. The _____ provides a uniform system of measuring pollution levels for the major air pollutants. It is based on a scale devised by the United States Environmental Protection Agency (USEPA) to provide a way for broadcasts and newspapers to report air quality on a daily basis.

The _____ is reported as a number on a scale of 0 to 500 and is the air quality indicator.

a. Pollutant Standards Index
b. 1509 Istanbul earthquake
c. 1703 Genroku earthquake
d. 1700 Cascadia earthquake

18. A _____ describes one of a number of pieces of legislation relating to the reduction of smog and air pollution in general. The use by governments to enforce clean air standards has contributed to an improvement in human health and longer life spans. Critics argue it has also sapped corporate profits and contributed to outsourcing, while defenders counter that improved environmental air quality has generated more jobs than it has eliminated.

a. 1509 Istanbul earthquake
b. 1703 Genroku earthquake
c. 1700 Cascadia earthquake
d. Clean Air Act

19. The United States Clean Air Act describes legislation enacted by Congress to control air pollution on a national level. The first Clean Air Act was the Air Pollution Control Act of 1955, followed by the Clean Air Act of 1963, the Air Quality Act of 1967, the Clean Air Act Extension of 1970, and _____ in 1977 and 1990. Numerous state and local governments have enacted similar legislation, either implementing federal programs or filling in locally important gaps in federal programs.

a. 1509 Istanbul earthquake
b. 1700 Cascadia earthquake
c. Clean Air Act Amendments
d. 1703 Genroku earthquake

20. The _____ is the primary federal law in the United States governing water pollution. Commonly abbreviated as the _____, the act established the symbolic goals of eliminating releases to water of high amounts of toxic substances, eliminating additional water pollution by 1985, and ensuring that surface waters would meet standards necessary for human sports and recreation by 1983.

The principal body of law currently in effect is based on the Federal Water Pollution Control Amendments of 1972, which significantly expanded and strengthened earlier legislation.

a. Surface Mining Control and Reclamation Act
b. Rule of Capture
c. Toxic Substances Control Act
d. Clean Water Act

21. _____ is the physical, chemical and biological characteristics of water. It is most frequently used by reference to a set of standards against which compliance can be assessed. The most common standards used to assess _____ relate to drinking water, safety of human contact, and for health of ecosystems.

a. Hydraulic head
b. 1700 Cascadia earthquake
c. 1509 Istanbul earthquake
d. Water Quality

22. _____ is the removal of solids (sediment, soil, rock and other particles) in the natural environment. It usually occurs due to transport by wind, water, or ice; by down-slope creep of soil and other material under the force of gravity; or by living organisms, such as burrowing animals, in the case of bioerosion.

_____ is distinguished from weathering, which is the process of chemical or physical breakdown of the minerals in the rocks, although the two processes may occur concurrently.

a. AL 333
b. AASHTO Soil Classification System
c. Erosion
d. AL 129-1

Chapter 18. Environmental Law

23. The _____ is a United States law, passed by the United States Congress in 1976, that regulates the introduction of new or already existing chemicals. It grandfathered most existing chemicals, in contrast to the Registration, Evaluation and Authorization of Chemicals (REACH) legislation of the European Union. However, as explained below, the _____ specifically regulates polychlorinated biphenyl (PCB) products.
   a. Surface Mining Control and Reclamation Act
   b. Rule of Capture
   c. General Mining Act of 1872
   d. Toxic Substances Control Act

24. The _____ is an informal name for the supereon comprising the eons of the geologic timescale that came before the current Phanerozoic eon. It spans from the formation of Earth around 4500 Mya (million years ago) to the evolution of abundant macroscopic hard-shelled animals, which marked the beginning of the Cambrian, the first period of the first era of the Phanerozoic eon, some 542 Mya. It is named after the Roman name for Wales - Cambria - where rocks from this age were first studied.
   a. 1703 Genroku earthquake
   b. 1509 Istanbul earthquake
   c. 1700 Cascadia earthquake
   d. Precambrian

25. _____ is a term applied with regulations on limiting pollutant discharges with regard to the abatement strategy. Similar terms are best available techniques , best practicable means or best practicable environmental option. The term constitutes a moving targets on practices, since developing societal values and advancing techniques may change what is currently regarded as 'reasonably achievable', 'best practicable' and 'best available'.
   a. 1703 Genroku earthquake
   b. 1509 Istanbul earthquake
   c. Best available technology
   d. 1700 Cascadia earthquake

26. An _____ is the result of a sudden release of energy in the Earth's crust that creates seismic waves. They are recorded with a seismometer or the related and mostly obsolete Richter magnitude, with a magnitude 3 or lower _____ being mostly imperceptible and magnitude 7 causing serious damage over large areas.
   a. Earthquake
   b. AL 129-1
   c. AASHTO Soil Classification System
   d. AL 333

27. A _____ is a geological phenomenon which includes a wide range of ground movement, such as rock falls, deep failure of slopes and shallow debris flows, which can occur in offshore, coastal and onshore environments. Although the action of gravity is the primary driving force for a _____ to occur, there are other contributing factors affecting the original slope stability. Typically, pre-conditional factors build up specific sub-surface conditions that make the area/slope prone to failure, whereas the actual _____ often requires a trigger before being released.
   a. 1700 Cascadia earthquake
   b. Landslide
   c. Mass wasting
   d. 1509 Istanbul earthquake

28. The _____ is one of the most remote United States national park areas, located on the Seward Peninsula. The National Preserve protects a remnant of the Bering Land Bridge that connected Asia with North America more than 13,000 years ago during the Pleistocene ice age. The majority of this land bridge, once thousands of miles wide, now lies beneath the waters of the Chukchi and Bering Seas.
   a. 1703 Genroku earthquake
   b. 1509 Istanbul earthquake
   c. 1700 Cascadia earthquake
   d. Bering Land Bridge National Preserve

29. A _____, in biogeography, is an isthmus or wider land connection between otherwise separate areas, which allows terrestrial animals and plants to cross over and colonise new lands. They can be created by marine regression, in which sea levels fall, exposing shallow, previously submerged sections of continental shelf; or when new land is created by plate tectonics; or occasionally when the sea floor rises due to post-glacial rebound after an ice age.

a. 1703 Genroku earthquake
b. 1509 Istanbul earthquake
c. 1700 Cascadia earthquake
d. Land Bridge

Chapter 19. Land-Use Planning and Engineering Geology

1. _____ is a professional engineering discipline that deals with the design, construction and maintenance of the physical and naturally built environment, including works such as bridges, roads, canals, dams and buildings. _____ is the oldest engineering discipline after military engineering, and it was defined to distinguish non-military engineering from military engineering. It is traditionally broken into several sub-disciplines including environmental engineering, geotechnical engineering, structural engineering, transportation engineering, municipal or urban engineering, water resources engineering, materials engineering, coastal engineering, surveying, and construction engineering.
   a. 1700 Cascadia earthquake
   b. 1509 Istanbul earthquake
   c. 1703 Genroku earthquake
   d. Civil engineering

2. The _____ characterizes the scratch resistance of various minerals through the ability of a harder material to scratch a softer material. It was created in 1812 by the German mineralogist Friedrich Mohs and is one of several definitions of hardness in materials science. The method, however, is of great antiquity, having first been mentioned by Theophrastus in his treatise On Stones in ca 300 BC, followed by Pliny the Elder in his Naturalis Historia circa A.D.
   a. Mohs scale of mineral hardness
   b. 1703 Genroku earthquake
   c. 1509 Istanbul earthquake
   d. 1700 Cascadia earthquake

3. An _____ is the result of a sudden release of energy in the Earth's crust that creates seismic waves. They are recorded with a seismometer or the related and mostly obsolete Richter magnitude, with a magnitude 3 or lower _____ being mostly imperceptible and magnitude 7 causing serious damage over large areas.
   a. Earthquake
   b. AL 333
   c. AASHTO Soil Classification System
   d. AL 129-1

4. In geology, a _____ or _____ line is a planar fracture in rock in which the rock on one side of the fracture has moved with respect to the rock on the other side. Large _____s within the Earth's crust are the result of differential or shear motion and active _____ zones are the causal locations of most earthquakes. Earthquakes are caused by energy release during rapid slippage along a _____.
   a. Stack
   b. Streak
   c. Tarn
   d. Fault

5. A _____ is a special-purpose map made to show geological features.

The stratigraphic contour lines are drawn on the surface of a selected deep stratum, so that they can show the topographic trends of the strata under the ground. It is not always possible to properly show this when the strata are extremely fractured, mixed, in some discontinuities, or where they are otherwise disturbed.

   a. 1509 Istanbul earthquake
   b. 1703 Genroku earthquake
   c. Geologic map
   d. 1700 Cascadia earthquake

6. _____ is molten rock that is found beneath the surface of the Earth, and may also exist on other terrestrial planets. Besides molten rock, _____ may also contain suspended crystals and gas bubbles. _____ often collects in a _____ chamber inside a volcano. _____ is capable of intrusion into adjacent rocks, extrusion onto the surface as lava, and explosive ejection as tephra to form pyroclastic rock.
   a. Volcanic rock
   b. Pluton
   c. Laccolith
   d. Magma

Chapter 19. Land-Use Planning and Engineering Geology

7. In geology, _____ or _____ soil is soil at or below the freezing point of water (0 >°C or 32 >°F) for two or more years. Ice is not always present, as may be in the case of nonporous bedrock, but it frequently occurs and it may be in amounts exceeding the potential hydraulic saturation of the ground material. Most _____ is located in high latitudes (i.e. land in close proximity to the North and South poles), but alpine _____ may exist at high altitudes in much lower latitudes.
   a. 1703 Genroku earthquake
   b. 1700 Cascadia earthquake
   c. 1509 Istanbul earthquake
   d. Permafrost

8. _____ crater is a crater on Mars's moon Deimos. It is about 3km in diameter. _____ crater is named after Jonathan _____, who predicted the existence of the moons of Mars.
   a. 1509 Istanbul earthquake
   b. 1703 Genroku earthquake
   c. Swift
   d. 1700 Cascadia earthquake

9. The _____ is a classification used for most Western Hemisphere tropical cyclones that exceed the intensities of tropical depressions and tropical storms. The scale divides hurricanes into five categories distinguished by the intensities of their sustained winds. In order to be classified as a hurricane, a tropical cyclone must have maximum sustained winds of at least 74 mph (33 m/s; 64 kt; 119 km/h.)
   a. 1703 Genroku earthquake
   b. 1509 Istanbul earthquake
   c. 1700 Cascadia earthquake
   d. Saffir-Simpson Hurricane Scale

10. A _____ is a body of water, which forms as water collects in the lowest parts of the depression that forms between two strands of an active strike-slip fault . The relative motion of the two fault strands results in a stretching of the land between them, causing the land between them to sink.
   a. Sag pond
   b. Tectonites
   c. Crenulation
   d. Transform fault

11. The _____ was proposed by the Danish geological pioneer Nicholas Steno (1638-1686.) This principle states that layers of sediment are originally deposited horizontally. The principle is important to the analysis of folded and tilted strata.
   a. Cyclostratigraphy
   b. Key bed
   c. Bedrock
   d. Principle of Original Horizontality

12. The _____ is a key axiom based on observations of natural history that is a foundational principle of sedimentary stratigraphy and so of other geology dependent natural sciences: 'Sedimentary layers are deposited in a time sequence, with the oldest on the bottom and the youngest on the top.'

The principle was first proposed in the 11th century by the Persian geologist, Avicenna , and the law was later formulated more clearly in the 17th century by the Danish scientist Nicolas Steno.

While discussing the origins of mountains in The Book of Healing in 1027, Avicenna first outlined the principle of the superposition of strata.

   a. Chronostratigraphy
   b. Law of superposition
   c. Lichenometry
   d. Stage

Chapter 19. Land-Use Planning and Engineering Geology

13. Before the advent of absolute dating in the 20th century, archaeologists and geologists were largely limited to the use of the _____ techniques. It estimates the order of prehistoric and geological events determined by using basic stratigraphic rules, and by observing where fossil organisms lay in the geological record, often in horizontal, stratified bands of rocks present throughout the world.

Though _____ can determine the sequential order in which a series of events occurred, not when they occur, it is in no way inferior to radiometric dating; in fact, _____ by biostratigraphy is the preferred method in paleontology, and is in some respects more accurate (Stanley, 167-9.)

   a. Geologic record
   b. Global Standard Stratigraphic Age
   c. Law of superposition
   d. Relative dating

14. _____ is the principle that the same scientific laws and processes are constant throughout space and time. It applies specifically to sciences that require a long timescale such as geology, astronomy, and paleontology. It was first defined by Charles Lyell (1797 - 1875), who incorporated James Hutton's gradualism into the idea of _____.
   a. AL 333
   b. AASHTO Soil Classification System
   c. AL 129-1
   d. Uniformitarianism

15. _____ is a technique used to date materials, usually based on a comparison between the observed abundance of a naturally occurring radioactive isotope and its decay products, using known decay rates. It is the principal source of information about the absolute age of rocks and other geological features, including the age of the Earth itself, and can be used to date a wide range of natural and man-made materials. Together with stratigraphic principles, _____ methods are used in geochronology to establish the geological time scale.
   a. Lichenometry
   b. Geologic record
   c. Law of superposition
   d. Radiometric dating

16. _____ is the process of determining a specific date for an archaeological or palaeontological site or artifact. Some archaeologists prefer the terms chronometric or calendar dating, as use of the word 'absolute' implies a certainty and precision that is rarely possible in archaeology. _____ is usually based on the physical or chemical properties of the materials of artifacts, buildings, or other items that have been modified by humans.
   a. Uranium-lead dating
   b. AASHTO Soil Classification System
   c. Absolute dating
   d. Erathem

17. The _____ Era, is the most recent of the three classic geological eras and covers the period from 65.5 million years ago to the present. It is marked by the Cretaceous-Tertiary extinction event at the end of the Cretaceous that saw the demise of the last non-avian dinosaurs and the end of the Mesozoic Era. The _____ era is ongoing.
   a. 1703 Genroku earthquake
   b. Cenozoic
   c. 1509 Istanbul earthquake
   d. 1700 Cascadia earthquake

18. The _____ Era is one of three geologic eras of the Phanerozoic eon. The division of time into eras dates back to Giovanni Arduino, in the 18th century, although his original name for the era now called the '_____' was 'Secondary' (making the modern era the 'Tertiary'.)

The _____ was a time of tectonic, climatic and evolutionary activity. The continents gradually shifted from a state of connectedness into their present configuration; the drifting provided for speciation and other important evolutionary developments.

a. 1509 Istanbul earthquake
b. 1703 Genroku earthquake
c. 1700 Cascadia earthquake
d. Mesozoic

19. The _____ is the earliest of three geologic eras of the Phanerozoic eon. The _____ spanned from roughly 542 to 251 million years ago (ICS, 2004), and is subdivided into six geologic periods; from oldest to youngest they are: the Cambrian, Ordovician, Silurian, Devonian, Carboniferous, and Permian.

The _____ covers the time from the first appearance of abundant, soft-shelled fossils to the time when the continents were beginning to be dominated by large, relatively sophisticated reptiles and modern plants. The lower (oldest) boundary was classically set at the first appearance of creatures known as trilobites and archeocyathids.

a. 1700 Cascadia earthquake
b. 1703 Genroku earthquake
c. 1509 Istanbul earthquake
d. Paleozoic

20. The _____ Eon is the current eon in the geologic timescale, and the one during which abundant animal life has existed. It covers roughly 545 million years and goes back to the time when diverse hard-shelled animals first appeared.

a. 1700 Cascadia earthquake
b. Phanerozoic
c. 1509 Istanbul earthquake
d. 1703 Genroku earthquake

21. The _____ is an informal name for the supereon comprising the eons of the geologic timescale that came before the current Phanerozoic eon. It spans from the formation of Earth around 4500 Mya (million years ago) to the evolution of abundant macroscopic hard-shelled animals, which marked the beginning of the Cambrian, the first period of the first era of the Phanerozoic eon, some 542 Mya. It is named after the Roman name for Wales - Cambria - where rocks from this age were first studied.

a. 1700 Cascadia earthquake
b. 1703 Genroku earthquake
c. Precambrian
d. 1509 Istanbul earthquake

22. The _____ is a chronologic schema (or idealized model) relating stratigraphy to time that is used by geologists, paleontologists and other earth scientists to describe the timing and relationships between events that have occurred during the history of the Earth. The table of geologic time spans presented here agrees with the dates and nomenclature proposed by the International Commission on Stratigraphy, and uses the standard color codes of the United States Geological Survey.

Evidence from radiometric dating indicates that the Earth is about 4.570 billion years old.

a. 1700 Cascadia earthquake
b. 1509 Istanbul earthquake
c. 1703 Genroku earthquake
d. Geologic time scale

23. A _____ is a type of map characterized by large-scale detail and quantitative representation of relief, usually using contour lines in modern mapping, but historically using a variety of methods. Traditional definitions require a _____ to show both natural and man-made features.

The Canadian Centre for Topographic Information provides this definition of a _____:

Other authors define _____s by contrasting them with another type of map; they are distinguished from smaller-scale 'chorographic maps' that cover large regions, 'planimetric maps' that do not show elevations, and 'thematic maps' that focus on specific topics.

   a. 1509 Istanbul earthquake
   c. 1700 Cascadia earthquake

   b. 1703 Genroku earthquake
   d. Topographic map

24. In stratigraphy, _____ is the native consolidated rock underlying the surface of a terrestrial planet, usually the Earth. Above the _____ is usually an area of broken and weathered unconsolidated rock in the basal subsoil. The top of the _____ is known as rockhead and identifying this, via excavations, drilling or geophysical methods, is an important task in most civil engineering projects.

   a. Polystrate
   c. Bedrock

   b. Sequence stratigraphy
   d. Biozones

25. _____ is a geyser in Yellowstone National Park in the U.S. state of Wyoming.

The geyser is located on the Firehole River within the Upper Geyser Basin. The geyser shoots steam and water to heights of 75 feet (23 m) in an arch over the river.

   a. 1703 Genroku earthquake
   c. Riverside Geyser

   b. 1700 Cascadia earthquake
   d. 1509 Istanbul earthquake

26. _____ consists of photographs of Earth or other planets made by means of artificial satellites. First television image of Earth from space transmitted by the TIROS-1 weather satellite.

First satellite photographs of Earth were made August 14, 1959 by the US satellite Explorer 6. The first satellite photographs of the Moon might have been made on October 6, 1959 by the Soviet satellite Luna 3, on a mission to photograph the far side of the Moon.

   a. 1700 Cascadia earthquake
   c. Satellite imagery

   b. 1509 Istanbul earthquake
   d. 1703 Genroku earthquake

27. A _____ is flat or nearly flat land adjacent to a stream or river that experiences occasional or periodic flooding. It includes the floodway, which consists of the stream channel and adjacent areas that carry flood flows, and the flood fringe, which are areas covered by the flood, but which do not experience a strong current.

They generally contain unconsolidated sediments, often extending below the bed of the stream.

   a. 1700 Cascadia earthquake
   c. Floodplain

   b. 1509 Istanbul earthquake
   d. 1703 Genroku earthquake

28. _____ is similar to color photography, but each pixel acquires many bands of light intensity data from the spectrum, instead of just the three bands of the RGB color model. More precisely, it is the simultaneous acquisition of spatially coregistered images in many spectrally contiguous bands.

Some spectral images contain only a few image planes of spectral data, while others are better thought of as full spectra at every location in the image.

a. AL 333
b. Imaging spectroscopy
c. AL 129-1
d. AASHTO Soil Classification System

29. _____ is any particulate matter that can be transported by fluid flow, and which eventually is deposited.

They are most often transported by water (fluvial processes) transported by wind (aeolian processes) and glaciers. Beach sands and river channel deposits are examples of fluvial transport and deposition, though _____ also often settles out of slow-moving or standing water in lakes and oceans.

a. Fech fech
b. Sediment
c. Dry quicksand
d. Brickearth

30. A _____ is a type of mudflow or landslide composed of pyroclastic material and water that flows down from a volcano, typically along a river valley. The term '_____' originated in the Javanese language of Indonesia. They can be best described as volcanic mudflows. They may not necessarily be caused by volcanic activity, but at the very least do originate from some type of volcanism.

a. 1509 Istanbul earthquake
b. 1703 Genroku earthquake
c. 1700 Cascadia earthquake
d. Lahar

31. A _____ zone or _____ area is the interface between land and a stream. Plant communities along the river margins are called _____ vegetation, characterized by hydrophilic plants. _____ zones are significant in ecology, environmental management, and civil engineering because of their role in soil conservation, their biodiversity, and the influence they have on aquatic ecosystems.

a. 1509 Istanbul earthquake
b. 1703 Genroku earthquake
c. Riparian
d. 1700 Cascadia earthquake

ANSWER KEY

Chapter 1
1. b   2. d   3. a   4. c   5. c   6. d   7. a   8. d   9. d   10. c
11. a   12. c   13. b   14. a   15. a   16. d   17. d   18. c   19. d   20. d
21. d   22. a   23. d   24. d   25. d   26. d   27. d   28. a   29. d   30. d

Chapter 2
1. a   2. b   3. a   4. d   5. d   6. d   7. b   8. a   9. b   10. a
11. d   12. b   13. d   14. d   15. a   16. d   17. c   18. d   19. b   20. d
21. a   22. d   23. c   24. c   25. c   26. b   27. a   28. a   29. d   30. d
31. d   32. d   33. c   34. c   35. b   36. d   37. d   38. d   39. d   40. c
41. d   42. d   43. d   44. d   45. c   46. b   47. d   48. d   49. d   50. b
51. c   52. d   53. b   54. a   55. b   56. c   57. a   58. b   59. b   60. d
61. b   62. d

Chapter 3
1. a   2. d   3. d   4. d   5. d   6. a   7. b   8. a   9. b   10. a
11. d   12. a   13. c   14. b   15. d   16. b   17. d   18. d   19. c   20. d
21. d   22. d   23. d   24. d   25. d   26. d   27. b   28. c   29. a   30. b
31. d   32. d   33. d   34. a   35. d   36. d   37. b   38. d   39. d   40. d
41. d   42. c   43. d   44. a   45. d   46. a   47. d

Chapter 4
1. a   2. a   3. c   4. d   5. a   6. d   7. a   8. d   9. a   10. a
11. d   12. d   13. a   14. d   15. d   16. d   17. d   18. b   19. d   20. d
21. d   22. d   23. d   24. d   25. d   26. c   27. d   28. a   29. d   30. c
31. a   32. b

Chapter 5
1. b   2. d   3. d   4. a   5. d   6. a   7. a   8. d   9. c   10. c
11. b   12. d   13. d   14. d   15. c   16. d   17. b   18. d   19. d   20. d
21. c   22. b   23. a   24. a   25. d   26. d   27. c   28. b   29. d   30. d
31. d   32. d   33. d   34. d   35. d   36. a   37. d   38. d   39. d   40. d
41. b   42. d   43. d   44. d   45. d   46. d   47. d   48. d

Chapter 6
1. b   2. d   3. b   4. a   5. d   6. d   7. d   8. a   9. d   10. a
11. d   12. a   13. c   14. d   15. c   16. d   17. d   18. d   19. c   20. d
21. d   22. a   23. a   24. d   25. b   26. d   27. d   28. c

Chapter 7
1. d   2. b   3. d   4. d   5. b   6. d   7. d   8. a   9. a   10. d
11. c   12. d   13. d   14. a   15. b   16. d   17. a   18. d   19. d   20. d
21. a   22. d   23. d   24. d   25. b   26. b   27. d   28. d   29. c   30. a
31. d   32. c   33. a   34. c   35. d

Chapter 8
1. d	2. b	3. b	4. d	5. d	6. b	7. d	8. b	9. b	10. a
11. d	12. d	13. d	14. d	15. d	16. d	17. a	18. d	19. d	20. d
21. d	22. d	23. a	24. d	25. d	26. a	27. b	28. d	29. b	30. c

Chapter 9
1. b	2. b	3. b	4. b	5. d	6. d	7. c	8. a	9. b	10. a
11. a	12. d	13. d	14. d	15. a	16. d	17. b	18. c	19. c	20. c
21. d	22. b	23. c	24. d	25. d	26. b	27. d	28. b	29. c	30. c
31. d	32. a	33. c	34. c	35. d	36. a	37. d	38. c	39. d	40. d
41. d	42. d	43. c	44. d	45. c	46. d	47. d			

Chapter 10
1. c	2. d	3. b	4. d	5. b	6. a	7. d	8. d	9. c	10. c
11. d	12. b	13. d	14. c	15. d	16. d	17. c	18. d	19. c	20. c
21. c	22. d	23. c	24. d	25. d	26. d	27. d	28. b	29. d	30. a
31. c	32. b	33. a	34. c	35. d	36. b	37. d	38. d	39. d	40. d
41. d	42. d	43. c	44. d	45. c	46. d	47. a	48. a		

Chapter 11
1. a	2. d	3. a	4. d	5. d	6. d	7. a	8. d	9. b	10. b
11. b	12. b	13. d	14. d	15. a	16. a	17. a	18. d	19. d	20. d
21. d	22. c	23. a	24. d	25. c	26. c	27. d	28. c	29. d	30. b
31. b	32. d	33. d	34. d	35. a	36. d	37. a	38. d	39. b	40. d
41. d	42. a	43. c	44. d						

Chapter 12
1. d	2. d	3. d	4. a	5. b	6. c	7. d	8. d	9. d	10. d
11. a	12. d	13. d	14. a	15. d	16. d	17. d	18. d	19. b	20. a
21. c	22. a	23. a	24. c	25. d	26. b	27. b	28. d	29. d	30. d
31. a	32. b	33. c	34. d	35. d	36. d	37. b	38. c		

Chapter 13
1. d	2. d	3. d	4. d	5. c	6. d	7. d	8. d	9. d	10. b
11. d	12. c	13. c	14. d	15. b	16. c	17. a	18. d	19. c	20. c
21. d	22. d	23. d	24. d	25. c	26. b	27. d	28. a	29. d	30. d
31. d	32. d	33. b	34. d	35. d	36. a	37. d	38. d	39. d	40. b
41. b	42. c	43. b	44. d						

Chapter 14
1. d	2. b	3. b	4. d	5. d	6. a	7. b	8. d	9. c	10. b
11. d	12. d	13. d	14. d	15. c	16. b	17. b	18. a	19. b	20. b
21. c	22. d	23. d	24. d	25. d	26. d	27. d	28. c	29. d	

ANSWER KEY

Chapter 15
1. d	2. a	3. c	4. b	5. d	6. d	7. c	8. d	9. b	10. b
11. c	12. a	13. b	14. d	15. c	16. d	17. d	18. d	19. d	20. b
21. c	22. c	23. a	24. a	25. b	26. d	27. d	28. d	29. a	30. d
31. d	32. c	33. d	34. d	35. a	36. d	37. d			

Chapter 16
1. c	2. b	3. b	4. b	5. c	6. b	7. b	8. c	9. d	10. b
11. c	12. a	13. a	14. b	15. a	16. a	17. b	18. d	19. b	20. b
21. a	22. a	23. b	24. d	25. d	26. c	27. a	28. b	29. d	30. d
31. b	32. d	33. a	34. a	35. d	36. d	37. b			

Chapter 17
1. b	2. c	3. a	4. d	5. a	6. d	7. d	8. b	9. d	10. b
11. c	12. b	13. d	14. b	15. d	16. d	17. a	18. c	19. d	20. c
21. d									

Chapter 18
1. d	2. b	3. b	4. d	5. d	6. b	7. a	8. b	9. d	10. d
11. d	12. b	13. d	14. b	15. c	16. a	17. a	18. d	19. c	20. d
21. d	22. c	23. d	24. d	25. c	26. a	27. b	28. d	29. d	

Chapter 19
1. d	2. a	3. a	4. d	5. c	6. d	7. d	8. c	9. d	10. a
11. d	12. b	13. d	14. d	15. d	16. c	17. b	18. d	19. d	20. b
21. c	22. d	23. d	24. c	25. c	26. c	27. c	28. b	29. b	30. d
31. c